Contents

Improve Your Reading

Your

Reading

3rd Edition

By
Ron Fry

CAREER PRESS
3 Tice Road
P.O. Box 687
Franklin Lakes, NJ 07417
1-800-CAREER-1
201-848-0310 (NJ and outside U.S.)
FAX: 201-848-1727

IMPROVE YOUR READING, 3RD EDITION

Cover design by The Visual Group

Printed in the U.S.A. by Book-mart Press

To order this title, please call toll-free 1-800-CAREER-1 (NJ and Canada: 201-848-0310) to order using VISA or MasterCard, or for further information on books from Career Press.

Library of Congress Cataloging-in-Publication Data

Fry, Ronald W.
    Improve your reading / by Ron Fry. -- 3rd ed.
       p.   cm. -- (Ron Fry's how to study program)
    Includes index.
    ISBN 1-56414-232-9 (pbk.)
    1. Reading. 2. Reading comprehension.   I. Title. II. Series:
Fry, Ronald W. How to study program.
LB1050.F797   1996
428.4'071--dc20   96-15757
                                                  CIP

Foreword

Read on!

This year marks another major milestone in the near-decade long evolution of my ***How to Study Program***—the addition of two new titles (***Get Organized*** and ***Use Your Computer***) as well as the reissuance of new editions of ***How to Study*** (its fourth), ***Improve Your Writing***, ***Improve Your Reading***, ***Improve Your Memory*** and ***"Ace" Any Test*** (all in third editions). ***Take Notes*** and ***Manage Your Time***, both still available in second editions, were not updated this year.

Why are these books the best-selling series of study guides ever published? Why are they still so *needed*, not only by students but by their parents who want so badly for them to do well? Because virtually all of the conditions I've been writing and speaking about across the country since 1988 have remained...or gotten *worse:*

1. Despite modest recent improvements in test scores—in 1995, the average on the verbal portion of the SAT rose five points, math scores improved three points—U.S. students still score abysmally low compared to many other countries, especially on science and math tests.

2. Most parents, when polled, say improving our public schools is our nation's number one priority. Those same parents do *not* think public schools are doing a very good job teaching their kids much of anything.

3. Business leaders continue to complain that far too many entry-level job candidates can barely read, write, add or multiply. Many can't fill out job applications! As a result, businesses are spending billions to teach employees the basic skills everyone agrees they should have learned in school.

It's almost inevitable that these conditions will *continue to worsen*. In just the next four years (i.e., by the year 2000), 7 million kids will enter school, increasing the number of students in U.S. elementary and high schools to more than 50 million. This is an increase that rivals the one caused by the boomer generation.

Unfortunately for this new crop of students, the money to fund their education just isn't there. Given the current state of the federal budget and most states' situations, these students probably face budget *cuts* all around. Voters aren't exactly lining up at the polls to fund new schools and pay teachers higher salaries.

This means that the old problems that most affect students' ability to learn—overcrowded classrooms, lack of resources (especially computers and other new technologies), lack of qualified teachers—will continue to frustrate students who want to learn but need help.

As a result, the need for my nine books will, unfortunately, continue, since they offer exactly the help most students need and their parents demand.

So who are you?

A number of you are students, not just the high school students I always thought were my readers, but also college students (a rousing plug for their high school preparation) and *junior* high school students (which says something far more positive about their motivation and eventual success).

Many of you reading this are adults. Some of you are returning to school, and some of you are long out of school but have figured out that if you could learn *now* the study skills your teachers never taught you, you'd do better in your careers—especially if you were able to read what you need to faster...and retain it better and longer.

All too many of you are parents with the same lament: "How do I get Johnny to do better in school? He thinks *Calvin and Hobbes* is the height of literature."

I want to briefly take the time to address every one of the audiences for this book and discuss some of the factors particular to each of you:

If you're a high school student

You should be particularly comfortable with both the language and format of this book—its relatively short sentences and paragraphs, occasionally humorous (hopefully) headings and subheadings, a reasonable but certainly not outrageous vocabulary. I wrote it with you in mind!

If you're a junior high school student

I doubt you'll have trouble with the concepts or language in this book. Sixth, seventh and eighth grade is the perfect time to learn the different ways to read and the methods to better retain whatever you're reading. You're probably just discovering that *The Babysitter's Club* series is *not* what your parents or teachers had in mind when they encouraged you to read "the classics."

If you're a "traditional" college student...

...somewhere in the 18 to 25 age range, I would have hoped you had already mastered most, if not all, of the basic study skills, especially reading and writing. Since you haven't, please make learning, using and mastering all of the study skills covered in my *How to Study Program* an absolute priority.

Do not pass "Go." Do not go on a date. Take the time to learn these skills now. You may have been able to kid yourself that mediocre or even poor reading skills didn't stop you from finishing, perhaps even succeeding in, high school. I guarantee you will not be able to kid *anyone* in college. You must master all of the skills in this book to survive, let alone succeed.

If you're the parent of a student of any age

Your child's school is probably doing little if anything to teach him or her how to study. Which means he or she is not learning how to *learn*. And that means he or she is not learning how to *succeed*.

Should the schools be accomplishing that? Absolutely. After all, we spend $275 billion on elementary and secondary education in this country, *an average of $6,000 per student per year*.

We ought to be getting more for that money than possible graduation, some football cheers and a rotten entry-level job market.

What can parents do?

There are probably even more dedicated parents out there than dedicated students, since the first phone call at any of my radio or TV appearances comes from a sincere and worried parent asking, "What can I do to help my kid do better in school?" Okay, here they are, the rules for parents of students of any age:

1. **Set up a homework area.** Free of distraction, well lit, all necessary supplies handy.

2. **Set up a homework routine.** When and where it gets done. Same bat-time every day.

3. **Set homework priorities.** Actually, just make the point that homework *is* the priority—before a date, before TV, before going out to play, whatever.

4. **Make reading a habit**—for them, certainly, but also for yourselves, presuming it isn't already. Kids will inevitably do what you *do*, not what you *say* (even if you say *not* to do what you *do*). So if you keep nagging them to read while *you* turn on the eighth sitcom of the night, what message do you think you're giving them?

5. **Turn off the TV.** Or, at the very least, severely limit when and how much TV-watching is appropriate. This may be the toughest one. Believe me, I'm the father of a 7-year old. I know. Do your best.

6. **Talk to the teachers.** Find out what your kids are supposed to be learning. If you don't, you can't really supervise. You might even be teaching them things at odds with what the teacher's trying to do.

7. **Encourage and motivate**, but don't nag them to do their homework. It doesn't work.

8. **Supervise their work,** but don't fall into the trap of *doing* their homework.

9. **Praise them to succeed**, but don't overpraise them for mediocre work. Kids know when you're slinging it. Be wary of any school or teacher that is more worried about your kid's "self esteem" than her grades, skills and abilities. I'm not advocating the withdrawal of kudos for good work, but kids need to get the message that "you get what you pay for"; that you need to work hard to actually *earn* rewards. Horror stories about teachers giving out good grades, reducing standards or not assigning homework because they're afraid some of the kids will "feel bad" if they don't do well are exactly that—horrible, scary stories. Such tactics merely set kids up for *bigger* failures down the road in a world that puts a premium on your skills and abilities and doesn't seem to care how you "feel" about it.

10. **Convince them of reality.** (This is for older students.) Okay, I'll admit it's almost as much of a stretch as turning off the TV, but learning and believing that the real world will not care about their grades but measure them solely by what they know and what they can do is a lesson that will save many tears (probably yours). It's probably never too early to (carefully) let your boy or girl genius get the message that life is not fair. Which is why teaching them resilience and determination—so they'll pick themselves up, dust themselves off and try again when they fail—is paramount.

11. **If you can afford it, get your kid(s) a computer** and all the software they can handle. Many people have been saying it for years (including me) and there really is no avoiding it: Your kids, whatever their age, absolutely must master technology (computers) in order to survive, let alone succeed, in school and after school. There's even new empirical data to back up all the braying: A recent decade-long study has shown that kids who master computers learn faster and earn higher test scores.

The importance of your involvement

Don't for a minute underestimate the importance of *your* commitment to your child's success: Your involvement in your child's education is absolutely essential to his or her eventual success. The results of every study done in the last two decades about what affects a child's success in school demonstrate that only one factor *overwhelmingly* affects it, every time: parental involvement. Not the size of the school, the money spent per pupil, the number of language labs, how many of the students go on to college, how many great teachers there are (or lousy ones). All factors, yes. *But none as significant as the effect you can have.*

So please, take the time to read this book (and all of the others in the series, but especially *How to Study*) yourself. Learn what your kids *should* be learning (and which of the other subject-specific books in the series your child needs the most).

You can help tremendously, *even if you were not a great student yourself, even if you never learned great study skills.* You can learn now with your child—it will help her in school, and it'll help *you* on the job, whatever your field.

If you're a nontraditional student

If you're going back to high school, college or graduate school at age 25, 45, 65 or 85—you probably need the help these nine books offer more than anyone! Why? You may have been able to kid yourself that mediocre or even poor reading skills didn't stop you from finishing, perhaps even succeeding in, high school. I guarantee you will not be able to kid *anyone* in college. You must master all of the skills in this book to survive, let alone succeed. As much as I emphasize that it's rarely too early to learn good study habits, I must also emphasize that it's never too *late*.

If you're returning to school and attempting to carry even a partial load of courses while simultaneously holding down a job, raising a family, or both, there are some particular problems you face that you probably didn't the first time you were in school:

Time and money pressures. Let's face it, when all you had to worry about was going to school, it simply *had* to be easier than going to school, raising a family and working for a living simultaneously. (And it was!) Mastering all of the techniques of time management is even more essential if you are to effectively juggle your many responsibilities to your career, family, clubs, friends, etc., with your commitment to school. Money management may well be another essential skill, whether figuring out how to pay for child care (something you probably didn't have to worry about the last time you were in school) or how to manage all your responsibilities while cutting your hours at work to make time for school.

Self-imposed fears of inadequacy. You may well convince yourself that you're just "out of practice" with all this school stuff. You don't even remember what to do with a highlighter! While some of this fear is valid, most is not. The valid part is that you are returning to an academic atmosphere, one that you may not have visited for a decade or two. And it *is* different (which I'll discuss more below) than the "work-a-day" world. That's just a matter of adjustment and, trust me, it will take a matter of days, if not hours, to dissipate. I suspect what many of you are really fearing is that you just aren't in that school "mentality" anymore, that you don't "think" the same way. Or, perhaps more pertinent to this book, that the skills you need to succeed in school are rusty.

I think these last fears are groundless. You've been out there thinking and doing for quite a few years, perhaps very successfully, so it's really ridiculous to think school will be so different. It won't be. Relax. And while you may think your study skills are rusty, as we discussed earlier, you've probably been using them every day in your career. Even if I can't convince you, you have my ***How to Study Program***, your refresher course. It will probably teach you more about studying than you ever forgot.

Maybe you're worried because you didn't exactly light up the academic power plant the first time around. Well, neither did Edison or Einstein or a host of other relatively successful people. But then, you've changed rather significantly since those halcyon days of "boola boolaing," haven't you? Held a series of jobs, raised a family, saved money, taken on more and more responsibility? Concentrate on how much *more* qualified you are for school *now* than you were *then*!

Feeling you're "out of your element." This is a slightly different fear, the fear that you just don't fit in any more. After all, you're not 18 again. But then, neither are fully half the college students on campus today. That's right, fully 50 percent of all college students are older than 25. The reality is, you'll probably feel more in your element now than you did the first time around!

You'll see teachers differently. Probably a plus. It's doubtful you'll have the same awe you did the first time around. At worst, you'll consider teachers your equals. At best, you'll consider them younger and not necessarily as successful or experienced as you are. In either event, you probably won't be quite as ready to treat your college professors as if they were akin to God.

There *are* differences in academic life. It's slower than the "real" world, and you may well be moving significantly faster than its normal pace. When you were 18, an afternoon without classes meant a game of Frisbee. Now it might mean catching up on a week's worth of errands, cooking (and freezing) a week's worth of dinners and/or writing four reports due last week. Despite your own hectic schedule, do not expect campus life to accelerate in response. You will have to get used to people and systems with far less interest in speed.

Some random thoughts about learning

Learning shouldn't be painful and certainly doesn't have to be boring, though it's far too often both. However, it's not necessarily going to be wonderful and painless, either. Sometimes you actually have to work hard to figure something out or get a project done. That *is* reality.

It's also reality that everything isn't readily apparent or easily understandable. Tell yourself that's okay and learn to get past it. Heck, if you think you understand everything you've read the first time through, you're kidding yourself. Learning something slowly doesn't mean there's something wrong with you. It may be a subject that virtually everybody learns slowly. A good student doesn't panic when something doesn't seem to be getting through. He just takes his time, follows whatever steps apply and remains confident that the light bulb will inevitably go on.

Parents often ask me, "How can I motivate my teenager?" My initial response is usually to smile and say, "If I knew the answer to that question, I would have retired very wealthy quite some time ago." However, I think there *is* an answer, but it's not something *parents* can do, it's something you, the student, have to decide: Are you going to spend the school day interested and alert or bored and resentful?

It's really that simple. Why not develop the attitude that you have to go to school anyway, so rather than being bored or miserable while you're there, you might as well be active and learn as much as possible? The difference between a C and an A or B for many students is, I firmly believe, merely a matter of wanting to do better. As I constantly stress in interviews, inevitably you will leave school. And very quickly, you'll discover the premium is on what you know and what you can do. Grades won't count anymore, neither will tests. So you can learn it all now or regret it later.

How many times have you said to yourself, "I don't know why I'm bothering trying to learn this (calculus, algebra, geometry, physics, chemistry, history, whatever). I'll *never* use this again!"? I hate to burst bubbles, but unless you've got a patent on some great new fortune-telling device, you have *no clue* what you're going to need to know tomorrow or next week, let alone next year or next decade.

I've been amazed in my own life how things I did with no specific purpose in mind (except probably to earn money) turned out years later to be not just invaluable to my life or career but essential. How was I to know when I took German as my language elective in high school that the most important international trade show in book publishing, my field, was in Frankfurt...Germany? Or that the basic skills I learned one year working for an accountant (while I was writing my first book) would become essential when I later started four companies? Or how important basic math skills would be in selling and negotiating over the years? (Okay, I'll admit it: I haven't used a differential equation in 20 years, but, hey, you never know!)

So learn it *all*. And don't be surprised if the subject you'd vote "least likely to ever be useful" winds up being the key to your fame and fortune.

There are other study guides

Though I immodestly maintain my **How to Study Program** to be the most helpful to the most people, there are certainly lots of other purported study books out there. Unfortunately, I don't think many of them deliver what they promise. In fact, I'm actually getting mad at the growing number of study guides out there claiming to be "the sure way to straight As" or something of the sort. These are also the books that dismiss reasonable alternative ways to study and learn with, "Well, that never worked for me," as if that is a valid reason to dismiss it, as if we should *care* that it didn't work for the author.

Inevitably, these other books promote the authors' "system," which usually means what *they* did to get through school. This "system," whether basic and traditional or wildly quirky, may or may not work for you. So what do you do if "their" way of taking notes makes no sense to you? Or you master their highfalutin "Super Student Study Symbols" and still get Cs?

I'm not getting into a Dennis Miller rant here, but there are very few "rights" and "wrongs" out there in the study world. There's certainly no single "right" way to attack a multiple choice test or absolute "right" way to take notes. So don't get fooled into thinking there *is*, especially if what you're doing seems to be working for you. Don't change what "ain't broke" just because some self-proclaimed study guru claims what you're doing is all wet. Maybe he's all wet. After all, if his system works for you, all it *really* means is you have the same likes, dislikes, talents or skills as the author.

Needless to say, don't read *my* books looking for the Truth—that single, inestimable system of "rules" that works for everyone. You won't find it, 'cause there's no such bird. You *will* find a plethora of techniques, tips, tricks, gimmicks and what-have-you, some or all of which may work for you, some of which won't. Pick and choose, change and adapt, figure out what works for you. Because *you* are the one responsible for creating *your* study system, *not me*.

Yes, I'll occasionally point out "my way" of doing something. I may even suggest that I think it offers some clear advantages to all the alternative ways of accomplishing the same thing. That *doesn't* mean it's some carved-in-stone, deviate-from-the-sacred-Ron-Fry-study-path-under-penalty-of-a-writhing-death kind of rule.

I've used the phrase "Study smarter, not harder" as a sort of catch-phrase in promotion and publicity for the **How to Study Program** for nearly a decade. So what does it mean to you? Does it mean I guarantee you'll spend less time studying? Or that the least amount of time is best? Or that studying isn't ever supposed to be hard?

Hardly. It does mean that studying inefficiently is wasting time that could be spent doing other (okay, probably more *fun*) things and that getting your studying done as quickly and efficiently as possible is a realistic, worthy and *attainable* goal. I'm no stranger to hard work, but I'm not a monastic dropout who thrives on self-flagellation. I try not to work harder than I have to!

In case you were wondering

Before we get on with all the tips and techniques necessary to read better and with more comprehension, let me make two important points about all nine study books.

First, I believe in gender equality, in writing as well as in life. Unfortunately, I find constructions such as "he and she," "s/he," "womyn" and other such stretches to be sometimes painfully awkward. I have therefore attempted to sprinkle pronouns of both genders throughout the text.

Second, you will find many pieces of advice, lists, examples and other phrases and sections spread throughout two or more of the nine books. Certainly *How to Study*, which is an overview of all the study skills, necessarily contains, though in summarized form, some of each of the other eight books.

The repetition is unavoidable. While I urge everyone to read all nine books in the series, but especially *How to Study*, they *are* nine individual books. And many people only buy one of them. Consequently, I must include in each the pertinent material *for that topic*, even if that material is then repeated in a second or even a third book.

That said, I can guarantee that the nearly 1,200 pages of my *How to Study Program* contain the most wide-ranging, comprehensive and complete system of studying ever published. I have attempted to create a system that is usable, that is useful, that is practical, that is learnable. One that *you* can use—whatever your age, whatever your level of achievement, whatever your IQ—to start doing better in school, in work and in life *immediately*.

Ron Fry
May 1996

Chapter 1

Reading: the mother of all study skills

I think you'll find this is a book unlike any you've read before. And if you take the time to read it, I promise it will make everything else you have to read—whatever your student status, whatever your job, whatever your age—a lot easier to get through.

Why? Because I'm going to show you how to plow through *all* your reading assignments—whatever the subjects—better and faster...*and* how to remember *more* of what you read.

This book is *not* a gimmicky speed-reading method. It's not a spelling and grammar guide. Nor is it a lecture on the joys of reading. It's a *practical* guide, geared to *you*—a student of any age who isn't necessarily a poor reader, but who wants to get more from reading and do better in school and in life.

Improve Your Reading

Personally, I love to read: the classics, spy thrillers, sports magazines, the newspaper, the back of the cereal box. When bored, tired, relaxing or eating, I'll read just about anything handy, just to be able to read *something*.

But, believe me, just because I loved to read didn't mean it was easy for me to face some of those deadly textbook reading assignments. As a student, you inevitably will be required, as I was, to spend hours poring through ponderous, fact-filled, convoluted reading assignments for subjects that are required but not exactly up there on the "All-Time Favorites" list.

You may love reading for pleasure, but have trouble reading textbook assignments for certain subjects. You may get the reading done, but forget what you've read nearly as quickly as you read it. Or you just may hate the thought of sitting still to read *anything*. What*ever* kind of student you are—and whatever your level of reading skill—I've written this book to help you surmount your reading challenge, *whatever it may be.*

And that includes, for those of you long out of school, reading those nap-inducing business tomes, trade magazine articles and other work-related stuff that's rarely reader-friendly.

You'll learn what you *should* read—and what you don't *have* to. You'll discover how to cut down on the time you spend reading, how to identify the main idea in your reading, as well as the important details and how to remember more of what you read.

I'll show you different ways to read various types of books, from dry science texts to cumbersome classics.

Who knows? I might even convince you reading is fun!

When you're a *good* reader, the world is your oyster—you qualify for better schools, better jobs, better pay. Poor readers qualify for poor jobs and less fulfilling lives.

Ready to begin? Get motivated!

Any attempt to improve your reading must begin with motivation. Reading is not a genetic trait that is written in your DNA—there's no gene that makes you a good or bad reader like the ones that decide your hair or eye color. For the most part, reading is an *acquired* skill. A skill *you* can secure, grow and sharpen. You just have to *want* to.

Within this book, I will address a number of very practical techniques that are sure to increase your reading comprehension. But they are just *techniques*.

You'll invariably find them utterly useless if you are not motivated to read in the first place.

As the Nike commercial lambastes all of us weekend warriors—"Just Do It!" This attitude—not technique—is where the quest for improved reading begins. You must make reading a habit.

Good reader vs. poor reader

Look at the following comparison of a good reader and a poor reader as if you were some corporate hot shot who could hire just one of the individuals:

Good reader: You read for purpose. You've clearly defined your reason for reading—a question you want answered, facts you must remember, ideas you need to grasp, current events that affect you or just the pleasure of following a well-written story.

Poor reader: Yes, you read, but often have no real reason for doing so. You aimlessly struggle through assigned reading, with little effort to grasp the "message."

Good reader: You read and assimilate thought. You hear and digest the concepts and ideas communicated.

Poor reader: You get lost in the muddle of words, struggling to make sense of what the author is trying to say. You are often bored because you force yourself to read every word to "get the message"… which you don't.

Good reader: You read critically and ask questions to evaluate whether the author's arguments are reasonable or off-the-wall. You recognize biases and don't just "believe" everything you read.

Poor reader: You swallow everything you read—hook, line and sinker. You suffer from the delusion that everything in print is true, and are easily swayed from what you formerly believed to be true by any argument that sounds good.

Good reader: You read a variety of books, magazines and newspapers—not limiting your reading to a *Far Side* humor book. You enjoy all types of reading—fiction, poetry, biography, current events.

Poor reader: You're a one-track reader—you read the sports pages, comics or Gothic novels. Current events? You catch updates about your world from occasional TV news "sound bites."

Good reader: You enjoy reading and embrace it as an essential tool in your desire to better yourself.

Poor reader: You hate to read, deeming it a chore to be endured only when you have to. Reading is "boring."

Take a minute and ask yourself, who would *you* hire? Yes, you might hire Mr. Poor Reader…in some low-paying job. But would you ever put someone with such low-level skills in a responsible position?

At this point, I won't ask you to evaluate your own level of reading skills. Characterizing yourself as a "good" or "poor" reader was not the point of this exercise. What is important is to realize that Ms. Good Reader didn't spring full-blown from Zeus's cranium reading Shakespearean sonnets and quoting Winston Churchill. She learned to read the same way you and I did—with "See Spot run."

In time and through making reading a habit, Ms. Good Reader acquired and honed a skill that will open a world of opportunity to her.

Mr. Poor Reader, at some point, decided that being a good reader was not worth the effort and made *poor* reading his habit.

The good news is that being a poor reader is not a life sentence—you *can* improve your reading. The challenge is to find the motivation!

How fast can you understand?

> *When we read too fast or too slowly, we understand nothing.*
>
> —Pascal

Are you worried that you read too slowly? You probably shouldn't be—less-rapid readers are not necessarily less able. What counts is what you comprehend and remember. And like anything else, practice will probably increase your speed levels. If you must have a ranking, read the 500-word selection below from start to finish, noting the elapsed time on your watch. Score yourself as follows:

Under 30 seconds	very fast
31-45 seconds	fast
46-60 seconds	high average
61-89 seconds	average
90-119 seconds	slow
120 seconds or more	very slow

If you're like most members of the third estate, you wonder if there are any real differences between politicians who say they're liberal Democrats and those who say they're conservative Republicans. Aren't they all just a bunch of slick-talking, vote-seeking, pocket-lining, power-hungry egomaniacs bent on getting elected? Maybe some are, but they also tend to have basic philosophical differences guiding their slick-talking, vote-seeking, pocket-lining, power-hungry pursuit of office.

Let's look at some fundamental political, social and economic differences between these groups.

Conservatives tend to champion free enterprise, or limited governmental control of the economy. They make the argument that people should be rewarded for their hard work and shouldn't expect government handouts through the welfare system. They are also heavily into national defense, law enforcement and promotion of the fundamental values of family, God and country. (Makes you want to break out into several verses of the "Star Spangled Banner," doesn't it?)

Liberals take a more paternalistic view of government. It is the last and only hope for many members of society who have suffered at the unscrupulous or uncaring hands of others. They contend that business would run amuck, exploiting workers and consumers in every market exchange, if not for government oversight. They also tend to be more concerned that everyone in society has equal access to a fair share of the economic pie, regardless of race, creed, sex, religion, shoe size, bank account, eye color or planet of birth. Their hearts bleed for all.

These differences often place conservatives and liberals, Republicans and Democrats, on different sides of issues such as school prayer, environmental quality, welfare reform, worker safety, abortion, the death penalty, business regulation, sex education and, well, just about every other newsworthy topic over the past 10 gadzillion years.

Of course, some of you might claim to be registered Democrats, yet say you support school prayer and welfare reform, or contend you're a Republican but you sure as heck want clean air and water and are willing to fight for them. Does this make you schizophrenic or hypocritical? Not necessarily. In fact, there are few *truly* liberal Democrats or *absolutely* conservative Republicans who support, without questions, the "straight" party line. Many members of the third estate have a combination of liberal and conservative views...just like you.

Now answer the following questions *without referring back to the text:*

1. According to the author, which of the following do traditional Republicans *not* favor?

  A. School prayer
  B. Sex education
  C. Welfare reform
  D. Banning abortion

2. Republicans favor:

  A. Limited governmental control of the economy
  B. Free enterprise
  C. Both
  D. Neither

3. Democrats favor:

  A. Less stringent environmental laws
  B. Lower taxes
  C. Both
  D. Neither

4. The author is probably:

    A. A Democrat

    B. A Republican

    C. An independent

    D. A smart aleck

A good reader should be reading fast or very fast and have gotten at least four of the five questions correct.

You should only worry—and plan to do something about it—if you fall in the slow or very slow range and/or missed two or more questions. Otherwise, you are probably reading as fast as you need to and retaining most of what you read.

Again, the relationship between speed and comprehension is paramount: Read *too* fast and you may comprehend *less*; reading more slowly does not necessarily mean you're not grasping the material.

What decreases reading speed/comprehension

1. Reading aloud or moving your lips when you read.

2. Reading mechanically—using your finger to follow words, moving your head as you read.

3. Applying the wrong *kind* of reading to the material.

4. Lacking sufficient vocabulary.

There are several things you can do to improve these reading mechanics.

To increase your reading speed:

1. Focus your attention and concentration.
2. Eliminate outside distractions.
3. Provide for an uncluttered, comfortable environment.
4. Don't get hung up on single words or sentences, but *do* look up (in the dictionary) key words that you must understand in order to grasp an entire concept.
5. Try to grasp overall concepts rather than attempting to understand every detail.
6. If you find yourself moving your lips when you read (vocalization), practice reading with a pen or some other (non-toxic, non-sugary) object in your mouth. If it falls out while you're reading, you know you have to keep working!

To increase comprehension:

1. Try to make the act of learning sequential—comprehension is built by adding new knowledge to existing knowledge.
2. Review and rethink at designated points in your reading. Test yourself to see if the importance of the material is getting through.
3. If things don't add up, discard your conclusions. Go back, reread and try to find an alternate conclusion.
4. Summarize what you've read, rephrasing it in your notes, in your own words.

Most importantly, read at the speed that's comfortable for you. Though I *can* read extremely fast, I *choose* to read novels much more slowly so I can appreciate the author's word play. Likewise, any material that I find particularly difficult to grasp slows me right down. I read newspapers, popular magazines and the like very fast, seeking to grasp the information but not worrying about every detail.

Should you take some sort of speed reading course, especially if your current speed level is low?

Reading for speed has some merit—many people who are slow readers read as little as possible, simply because they find it so tedious and boring. But just reading faster is not the answer to becoming a good reader.

I can't see that such a course could particularly *hurt* you in any way. I can also, however, recommend that you simply keep practicing reading, which will increase your speed naturally.

Don't remember less...faster

Retention is primarily a product of what you understand. It has little to do with how *fast* you read, how great an outline you can construct or how many fluorescent colors you can mark your textbooks with. Reading a text, grasping the message and remembering it, are the fundamentals that make for high-level retention. Reading at a 1,000-word-per-minute clip does not necessarily mean that you have a clue as to what a text really says.

As you work toward improving your reading, realize that speed is secondary to comprehension. If you can read an assignment faster than anyone in class, but can't give a one-sentence synopsis of what you read, you lose. If you really get the author's message—even if it takes you an hour or two longer than some of your friends—your time will pay off in huge dividends in class and later in life.

That's why this book concentrates only on how you as a student can increase what you retain from your reading assignments. Whether you're reading a convoluted text-book that bores even the professor to tears or a magazine article, newspaper feature or novel, you follow a certain process to absorb what you've read, which consists of:

1. Grasping the main idea.
2. Gathering the facts.
3. Figuring out the sequence of events.
4. Drawing conclusions.

When you spend an hour reading an assignment, then can't recall what you've just read, it's usually because a link in this chain has been broken. You've skipped one of these crucial steps in your reading process, leaving your understanding of the material filled with gaps.

To increase your retention rate, you need to master *each level* in this chain of comprehension. Not everything you read will require that you comprehend on all four levels. Following a set of cooking directions, for example, simply requires that you discern the sequence for adding all ingredients. Other reading will demand that you are able to compile facts, identify a thesis and give some critical thought as to its validity.

Ms. Good Reader is not only able to perform at each level of comprehension, but also has developed an instinct: She recognizes that certain things she reads can be read *just* to gather facts or *just* to grasp the main idea. She then is able to read quickly to accomplish this goal and move on to her next assignment—or to that Steven King novel she's been dying to read.

This book will help you develop a sense of what is involved in *each* step of the reading process.

The first chapters will address these different steps and provide exercises designed to help you master each stage in the process of retaining what you read.

In the final chapters, we will look at how to read literature, how to read a math or science textbook and how to outline so that you can easily review a text.

By the time you finish this short book, you should find that by following the procedures I've suggested, you have significantly improved your reading comprehension.

Finding other textbooks

Few textbooks are written by what most of us would even remotely call professional writers. While the authors and editors might well be experts, even legends, in a particular subject, writing in jargon-free, easy-to-grasp-prose is probably not their strong suit. You will occasionally be assigned a textbook that is so obtuse you aren't even sure whether to read it front to back, upside down or inside out.

If you find a particular chapter, section or entire textbook as tough to read as getting your baby brother to do you a favor, get to the library or the bookstore and find *another* book covering the *same* subject area that you *can* understand. (You might even consider asking your teacher or professor for recommendations. He or she will probably make your job of finding a *readable* text a lot easier. You may even score some brownie points for your seeming initiative (as long as you don't wonder aloud what caused him or her to select that torturous text in the first place!).

"Ron," I hear you grumbling, "what happened to the 'study smarter, not harder' bit? This can't *possibly* be a time saver. Heck, I'll bet the books don't even cover the subject in the same way, let alone follow the same sequence! I'll be stuck slogging through *two* books."

All true, possibly. But if you just don't get it, maybe it's because the *author* just doesn't know how to *explain* it. *Maybe it's not your fault!* Too many students have sweated, moaned, dropped classes, even changed majors because they thought they were dumb, when it's possible it's the darned textbook that's dense, not you. So instead of continuing to slog though the mire, find an expert who can actually write—they're out there—and learn what you need to. After finally understanding the subject by reading this other text, you'll find much of the original textbook much easier to use...presuming you need it at all.

Answers to quiz: B, C, D, D.

Chapter 2

Reading with purpose

Even if you consider yourself "not much of a reader," you read *something* each and every day: A magazine article, instructions for hooking up the VCR, telephone messages tacked on the refrigerator, notes from your latest heartthrob.

Regardless of *what* you are reading, you have a purpose that dictates *how* you are going to read it—and you read different items in different ways. You wouldn't read the VCR instructions as you would a novel, any more than you'd read the magazine article in the same way as a grocery list. Without a purpose, you'd find yourself reading aimlessly and very inefficiently.

Unfortunately, many of the students I've talked to have not yet realized the importance of having a purpose for reading. Their lack of reading purpose can be summed up by the proverb, "If you aim at nothing, you will hit the bullseye every time."

Before you can understand what you're reading—and *remember* it—you must know *why* you're reading it in the first place.

Defining your purpose for reading

What is your purpose in reading? If the best answer you can come up with is, "Because my teacher said so," we need to come up with some better reasons. Reading a chapter just so you can say, "I finished my assignment," is relatively futile. You may as well put the book under a pillow and hope to absorb it by osmosis.

Unless you identify some purpose to read, you will find yourself flipping the pages of your textbooks while seldom retaining anything more than the chapter titles.

According to reading experts, there are six fundamental purposes for reading:

1. To grasp a certain message.
2. To find important details.
3. To answer a specific question.
4. To evaluate what you are reading.
5. To apply what you are reading.
6. To be entertained.

Because reading with purpose is the first step toward improved comprehension, let me suggest some simple techniques you can use to identify a purpose for *your* textbook reading.

Find the clues in every book

There is a group of special sections found in nearly all textbooks and technical materials (in fact, in almost all books except novels) that contain a wealth of information and can help you glean more from your reading. Becoming familiar with this data will enrich your reading experience and often make it easier. Here's what to look for:

The first page after the title page is usually the *table of contents*—a chapter-by-chapter list of the book's contents. Some are surprisingly detailed, listing every major point or topic covered in each chapter.

The first prose section (after the title page, table of contents and, perhaps, *acknowledgments page*, in which the author thanks other authors, his editor, researcher, friends, relatives, teachers, etc., most of which you can ignore), the *preface,* is usually a description of what information you will find in the book. Authors may also use the preface to point out unique aspects of their books.

The *introduction* may be in place of or in addition to the preface and may be written by the author or some "name" the author has recruited to lend additional prestige to his or her work. Most introductions are an even more detailed overview of the book—chapter-by-chapter summaries are often included to give the reader a feel for the material to be covered.

Footnotes may be found throughout the text (a slightly elevated number following a sentence, quotation, etc., e.g., "jim-dandy"[24]) and either explained at the bottom of the page on which they appear or in a special section at the back of the text. Footnotes may be used to cite sources of direct quotes or ideas and/or to further explain a point, add information, etc., outside of the text. You may make it a habit to ferret out sources cited for further reading.

If a text tends to use an alarmingly high number of terms with which you may not be familiar, the considerate author will include a *glossary*—essentially an abridged dictionary that defines all such terms.

The *bibliography*, usually at the end of the book, may include the source material the author used to research the textbook, a list of "recommended reading," or both. It is usually organized alphabetically by subject, making it easy for you to go to your library and find more information on a specific topic.

Appendices containing supplementary data or examples relating to subject matter covered in the text may also appear in the back of the book.

The last thing in a book is usually the *index*, an alphabetical listing that references, by page number, every mention of a particular name, subject, topic, etc., in the text.

Making it a habit to utilize all of these tools in your textbook can only make your studying easier.

Look for the clues in each chapter

Every textbook offers some clues that will help you define a purpose for reading. Begin with a very quick overview of the assignment, looking for questions that you'd like answered. Consider the following elements of your reading assignment *before* you begin your reading.

Much like the headlines of a newspaper clue you into what the story is about, these elements will give insight into what the section or chapter is trying to communicate:

Chapter heads and subheads

Chapter titles and bold-faced subheads announce the detail about the main topic. And, in some textbooks, paragraph headings or bold-face "lead-ins" announce that the author is about to provide finer details.

So start each reading assignment by going through the chapter, beginning to end, *reading only the bold-faced heads and subheads.*

For example, suppose you encountered the heading, "The Demise of the American Indian," in your history text. You might use it to form the following questions:

A. *What* caused the demise of the American Indian?

B. *Who* caused it?

C. *When* did it occur?

D. *Why* did it occur?

As you read the chapter, you'll find yourself seeking answers to these questions. You now have a purpose!

Often you may find headings that contain words or terms you don't recognize. Seeking to define these terms or explain a concept should then define your purpose.

This process of headline reading takes only a few minutes, but it lays the groundwork for a more intelligent and efficient reading of the chapter. You'll have some idea where the author is headed, which will give you a greater sense of what the most important details are and clarify where you should be concentrating your studying.

End-of-chapter summaries

If you read a mystery from start to finish, the way the author hopes you will, you're likely to get thrown off the scent by "red herrings" and other common detective novel devices. However, if you read the last page first, knowing the outcome will help you detect how the author constructed the novel and built an open-and-shut case for his or her master sleuth. You'd perceive a wealth of details about the eventually unmasked murderer that might have gone *un*noticed had he been just another of the leading suspects.

Similarly, knowing what the author is driving at in a *textbook* will help you look for the important building blocks for his conclusions while you're reading.

It may not be fun to read a mystery novel this way, but when it comes to textbook reading, it will help you define your purpose for reading. And further, it will transform you into a much more *active* reader, making it less likely you'll doze off while being beaten senseless by the usual ponderous prose.

Pictures, graphs and charts

Most textbooks, particularly those in the sciences, will have charts, graphs, numerical tables, maps and other illustrations. All too many students see these as fillers—padding to glance at quickly, and, just as quickly, forget.

If you're giving these charts and graphs short shrift, you're really shortchanging *yourself.* Be sure to observe how they supplement the text, what points they emphasize and make note of these.

Highlighted terms, vocabulary and other facts

In some textbooks, you'll discover that key terms and information are highlighted within the body text. (I don't mean highlighted by a previous student—consider such yellow-markered passages with caution!) To find the definitions of these terms, or to find the application of facts may then be your purpose for reading.

Questions

Some textbook publishers use a format in which key points are emphasized by questions, either within the body or at the end of the chapter. If you read these questions *before* reading the chapter, you'll have a better idea of what material you need to pay closer attention to.

Prereading your assignment

If you begin your reading assignment by seeking out these heads, subheads and other purpose-finding elements of the chapter, you'll have completed your prereading step. What is prereading? It is simply beginning your assigned reading by reviewing these clues and defining your purpose (or purposes) for reading.

I advise that you *always* preread every assignment! Why? Have you ever spent the better part of an evening plowing through an assignment only to finish with little or no understanding of what you just read? If the answer is yes, then you probably failed to preread it.

Reading faster without speed reading

While the heads, subheads, first sentences and other author-provided hints we've talked about will help you get a quick read on what a chapter's about, some of the *words* in that chapter will help you concentrate on the important points and ignore the unimportant. Knowing when to speed up, slow down, ignore or really concentrate will help you read both faster *and* more effectively.

When you see words like "likewise," "in addition," "moreover," "furthermore" and the like, you should know nothing new is being introduced. If you already know what's going on, speed up or skip what's coming entirely.

On the other hand, when you see words like "on the other hand," "nevertheless," "however," "rather," "but" and their ilk, slow down—you're getting information that adds a new perspective or contradicts what you've just read.

Lastly, watch out for "payoff" words such as, "to summarize," "in conclusion," "therefore," "consequently," "thus"—especially if you only have time to "hit the high points" of a chapter or you're reviewing for a test. Here's where the real meat is, where everything that went before is happily tied up in a nice bow and ribbon, a present that enables you to avoid having to unwrap the entire chapter.

Purpose defines reading method

Typically, your purpose for reading dictates how you read. There are basically three types of reading we all do:

1. **Quick reference reading** focuses on seeking specific information that addresses a particular question or concern we might have.
2. **Critical reading** involves discerning ideas and concepts that require a thorough analysis.
3. **Aesthetic or pleasure reading**, is what we do for sheer entertainment or to appreciate an author's style and ability.

As you define your purpose for reading, you will determine which method of reading is necessary to accomplish this purpose. In the following table are some examples of types of reading, why you might read them and the method you should use:

Type	Purpose	Method
Newspaper advertisement	To locate best price for car	Quick reference
Magazine	To stay aware of current events	Quick reference
Self-help book	To learn to get along better with your family	Critical
Biology text	To prepare for an exam	Critical
New issue of *Rolling Stone*	To take your mind off biology!	Pleasure

If you're a good reader or desire to be one: You will always fit your reading *method* to your reading *purpose;* you have trained or are training yourself in a variety of reading skills; you have no problem switching your method to accommodate your purpose; and you are unsatisfied reading only one type of material.

A poor reader, on the other hand, reads everything the same way—doggedly plowing through the biology assignment, the newspaper and the Stephen King novel...word by painful word. Reading with purpose is both foreign and foreboding to such a person, which makes it difficult for him or her to adapt a method of reading.

Become an active reader

Reading with purpose is as vital to your comprehension and retention as oxygen is to life. It is the cornerstone of *active* reading, reading that involves thinking—that process of engaging your mind and emotions in what the author is trying to communicate. Too many readers seek to absorb information passively as their eyes move across the page. The active reader *involves* him- or herself in receiving a message—a fact, an idea, an opinion—that is readily retained because he or she had a *purpose*.

Following is a passage adapted from *Make the Most of Your Workday* by Jonathan and Susan Clark (Career Press, 1994). *Preread* the passage in order to determine a *purpose* for reading. Be sure to use the note page following to jot down questions that may have been raised through your preread, and the purpose:

Are You Really Trying to Do Too Much?

We all need checks and balances to manage life's resources and responsibilities, and that's what this chapter is all about. You may be overloaded with responsibilities and demands. You may feel incapable of effectively organizing and managing all of your projects. You may be hoping for a mixture of ideas and solutions that, blended together, can restore a feeling of control.

It's possible that all your concerns about your time boil down to one simple fact: You may simply be trying to do too much!

The best organized schedule, the most well-planned "Daily Action Plan," the most effectively applied list of 10 steps or 12 ideas, cannot change your situation if you are trying to accomplish more than you have time to do.

How can you determine if self-overload conditions already exist? What can you do to change those conditions? Generally speaking, if you feel overloaded, you *are* overloaded. If you *don't* feel that you're presently overloaded, you may fear that you're heading that way...fast. Your question then is, "How can I keep this from happening?"

Whether you've already reached the breaking point or see the point approaching fast, to avoid certain demise you must take a long, hard look at all of your commitments and activities. You must be honest and realistic.

The very first step is to ask yourself: "If I were not already doing this, would I choose to get involved?"

A case study

Jim North, a personnel director for a small manufacturing firm, began attending monthly meetings of a local organization of personnel directors.

Although Jim enjoyed the association with other professionals in his field, he found it difficult to attend the breakfasts every month. He frequently got his most productive work done early in the day, and sometimes the meetings seemed to have only marginal professional benefits, since a number of the members seemed mainly interested in the meeting as a social occasion.

Jim was surprised when Gerry Duckworth, a member he knew only casually, called one day and asked if he would consider running for vice president of the organization for the coming year. When Jim asked what the position involved, Gerry said, "Oh, you really don't have to do anything. We just need someone to hold that office."

As it turned out, Jim's was the only name placed in nomination, and he was elected to the office.

A few days later, Kathy Cornell, the president, called Jim and told him there was a lunch meeting scheduled later that week for all the officers of the organization.

When Jim went to the officers' meeting, he discovered that the vice president had numerous responsibilities, including planning the programs for the breakfasts each month and heading up the annual new members campaign. Kathy excitedly told the group that she had just learned her company was sending her across the country for three months to oversee the opening of a new office. This meant Jim would function as president for that time!

Jim obviously realized this new job was a lot bigger than he had been told it was. If he had known it entailed so much responsibility, he probably would have declined the nomination. He began to envision the additional hours and energy required (which he really didn't have) to serve an organization of questionable value to him, and felt overwhelmed. He also found himself feeling resentful that the importance of the job had been misrepresented to him.

What was Jim's biggest mistake? If you were Jim, what would you do now?

What actually happened

Jim quickly reassessed his own priorities and determined that this new responsibility didn't fit into them. He analyzed what impact giving up that much additional time and energy would have on the activities to which he had already committed. He wondered how much more he could do in those areas if he were to direct the same time and energy to his priorities.

At the end of the meeting, he asked Kathy to stay for a few minutes. Then he told her: "Kathy, if I had realized the scope of this job, I never would have agreed to serve. I'm sorry I didn't ask more questions when Gerry called, and I realize this will put the association in a temporary bind, but I'm going to have to resign from the office."

Kathy reluctantly accepted Jim's resignation. She appointed another vice president before the next meeting and made the announcement in the chapter's newsletter.

For a few months, Jim felt a little uncomfortable at the meetings. A few people teased him about "chickening out" of the job, but the teasing eventually stopped. When the election of officers came around the next year, Jim reflected gratefully on his decision, realizing he had been wise to put his efforts into his priorities.

What it all meant to Jim

Jim could have decided to make the best of his position and plan great programs and spearhead an enthusiastic member campaign. Maybe he would have even gotten more out of the meetings and his opportunities to network with the other members of the chapter.

But sometimes people simply spread themselves too thin—trying to do too much and please too many people. When you identify your priorities by asking, "What's important to me?" it's often far more satisfying and rewarding to redirect additional time and effort to previous commitments than to add even more activities to an already jammed calendar.

And what it means to you

Put yourself in this story. Change the situation to one you're facing. Wouldn't you really rather be out from under this responsibility than trying to juggle it and fit it in with other, more important matters? Won't you feel good when that commitment is no longer on your list?

Remember, for any project that you're already involved in or are thinking about taking on, ask yourself this question: "Can I make a strong personal commitment to invest my time and abilities in this purpose, project or pursuit?" If the answer is "I can't make a full commitment," then it's best not to start it or, if already involved, to find a way out.

Your notes

What clues can you find that help you define a purpose for reading this passage?

_____

_____

_____

_____

_____

_____

What purpose or purposes did you determine for reading this passage?

_____

_____

_____

_____

_____

_____

What method, based on your purpose, would you use to read this passage?

_____

_____

_____

_____

_____

_____

_____

_____

_____

Chapter 3

Finding the main idea

In all good writing, there is a controlling thesis or message that connects all of the specific details and facts. This concept or idea is usually expressed as a generalization that summarizes the entire text.

Good comprehension results when you are able to grasp this main message, even if you sometimes forget some of the details. When you understand the intent, you have a context in which to evaluate the reasoning, the attitude and whether the evidence cited really is supportive of the conclusions drawn.

An obsession for facts can obscure the "big picture," giving you an understanding of the trees but no concept of the forest. How many of you have spent hours studying for an important exam, collecting dates, names, terms and formulas, but failed to ferret out the main idea, the underlying concept that is composed of these facts?

In longer, more involved readings, many messages are combined to form a chain of thought, which, in turn, may or may not be communicating one thesis or idea.

Your ability to capture this chain of thought determines your level of comprehension—and what you retain.

Dissecting your reading assignment

To succeed in identifying the main idea in any reading assignment, you must learn to use these helpful tools:

1. The topic sentence of a paragraph.
2. Summary sentences.
3. Supporting sentences.
4. Transitional statements.

As you learn to dissect your reading assignment paragraph by paragraph, identifying its many parts and their functions, you'll grasp the main idea much more quickly—and remember it much longer.

Recognizing a topic sentence

Every paragraph has a *topic sentence*—the sentence that summarizes what the paragraph is about. Even if a paragraph does not have such a clearly stated sentence, it can be implied or inferred from what is written.

Generally, the topic sentence is the first or last sentence of a paragraph—the one statement that announces, "Here's what this paragraph is all about!"

When the topic sentence is obscured or hidden, you may need to utilize two simple exercises to uncover it:

1. Pretend you're a headline writer for your local newspaper—write a headline for the paragraph you just read.
2. Write a five-word summary describing what the paragraph is about.

Exercise: identifying a topic sentence

Write a headline or five-word summary for each of the following paragraphs:

It's very exciting to venture through display homes or visit open houses and dream of moving in. Just remember to treat home buying or selling very seriously and take time for a reality check now and then. This is a decision you'll live with for many years. "Home"-work is the key. Knowing the numbers ahead of time and setting your limits will definitely pay off.

More than ever, we are looking for meaning, fulfillment and personal growth in our lives. And we're demanding those qualities in our jobs and business as well. An organization that understands this tends to have a happier and more productive workforce. If an organization has a clearly articulated statement of philosophy and values, there can be a meshing of corporate and personal goals known as *alignment*.

Like it or not, government is with us and will be for a long time to come. One can't even imagine a society that would not involve some sort of government. In that numerous needs-satisfying goods are produced only by the government, we have no choice but to keep it around. And because we have it, we have to pay taxes. The question then is whether our tax dollars are spent wisely. No. They aren't and they never will be, because government is incredibly inefficient and incompetent. The problem is, if the government doesn't perform duties badly, they probably won't be performed at all.

As you can see from these three paragraphs, the topic sentence is not always clearly stated. This is especially true in a number of the convoluted textbooks all of us have read. When trying to discern the main idea of such writing, you may need a more in-depth analysis.

You can begin your analysis by turning, once again, to our helpful questions. Is the passage written to address one of the questions?

1. **Who?** The paragraph focuses on a particular person or group of people. The topic sentence tells you *who* this is.

2. **When?** The paragraph is primarily concerned with *time*. The topic sentence may even begin with the word "when."

3. **Where?** The paragraph is oriented around a particular place or location. The topic sentence states *where* you are reading about.

4. **Why?** A paragraph that states reasons for some belief or happening usually addresses this question. The topic sentence answers *why* something is true or *why* an event happened.

5. **How?** A paragraph that identifies the way something works or the means by which something is done. The topic sentence explains the *how* of what is described.

You will notice that I didn't include the question "What?" in this list. This is not an oversight. "What?" addresses such a broad range of possibilities that asking this question will not necessarily lead you to the topic sentence.

The best test to determine whether you have identified the topic sentence is to rephrase it as a question. If the paragraph answers the question that you've framed, you've found the topic sentence.

Summary, support or transitional?

Another technique that will lead you to the topic sentence is to identify what purpose *other* sentences in the paragraph serve—kind of a process of elimination.

Generally, sentences can be characterized as *summary, support* or *transitional*.

Summary sentences state a general idea or concept. As a rule, a topic sentence is a summary sentence—a concise yet inclusive statement that expresses the general intent of the paragraph. (By definition, the topic sentence is never a support sentence.)

Support sentences provide the specific details and facts that give credibility to the author's points of view. They give examples, explain arguments, offer evidence or attempt to prove something as true or false. They are not meant to state generally what the author wants to communicate—they are intended to be specific, not conceptual, in nature.

Transitional sentences move the author from one point to another. They may be viewed as bridges connecting the paragraphs in a text, suggesting the relationship between what you just finished reading and what you are about to read. Good readers are attuned to the signals such sentences provide—they are buzzers that scream, "This is what you are going to find out next!"

Transitional sentences may also alert you to what you should have just learned. Unlike support sentences, transitional sentences provide invaluable and direct clues to identifying the topic sentence.

Some examples of transitional signals

Any sentence that continues a progression of thought or succession of concepts is a transitional sentence. Such a sentence may begin with a word such as "first," "next," "finally" or "then" and indicate the before/after connection between changes, improvements or alterations.

Transitional sentences that begin in this way should raise these questions in your mind:

1. Do I know what the previous examples were?

2. What additional example am I about to learn?

3. What was the situation prior to the change?

Other transition statements suggest a change in argument or thought or an exception to a rule. These will generally be introduced by words like "but," "although," "though," "rather," "however" or similar conjunctions that suggest an opposing thought.

Such words ought to raise these questions:

1. What is the gist of the argument I just read?

2. What will the argument I am about to read state?

3. To what rule is the author offering an exception?

In your effort to improve your reading, developing the ability to recognize the contrast between general, inclusive words and statements (summary sentences) and specific, detail-oriented sentences (transitional or support sentences) is paramount.

Taking notes

The final step toward grasping and retaining the main idea of any paragraph is taking notes. There are several traditional methods students employ—outlining, high-lighting, mapping and drawing concept trees.

An exhaustive review of all these methods is not within the scope of this particular book, but for a complete discussion of note-taking techniques, be sure to read **Take Notes**, another of the nine books in my **How to Study Program.**

Whichever method you employ to retain the main idea, focus on the topic sentences, not on the specific details.

If you are a highlighter—you enjoy coloring textbooks with fluorescent markers—you will want to assign one color that you will always use to highlight topic sentences. Avoid what too many students do—highlighting virtually every paragraph. This practice will just extend your review time considerably—you'll find yourself rereading instead of reviewing.

If you utilize outlining or mapping (diagramming what you read rather than spending time worrying about Roman numerals and whether to use lower case letters or upper case letters on certain lines) you will find that your time will best be spent writing five-word summaries of the topic sentences.

If you find yourself getting bogged down in details and specifics, you are wasting valuable time. Again, writers are using these details to communicate their concepts—they are not necessarily to be remembered.

Read the following passage from *Economic Literacy* by Orley M. Amos, Jr. (Career Press, 1994), seeking out the topic sentences. Then summarize the main idea or ideas in five-word phrases.

An Altogether Look at Unions

Unions are organizations of workers—in the same industry, working for the same company, or in the same occupation—that negotiate with their employers over things like wages, fringe benefits, working conditions, hiring and firing procedures and other job-related items. The formal negotiation, where the union and the company seek to work out a contractual agreement on these various issues is termed *collective bargaining*.

In recent years, most of these collective bargaining agreements have been pretty straightforward. Unions demand a few things, companies return with their "best" offers, then they haggle back and forth until they reach a compromise. If this sounds a lot like buying a car or house, it is. It's the same sort of one-on-one negotiation that takes place in many markets.

While the sorts of things that unions and management do to each other might appear childish, they have a serious and violent history. Their confrontations are as fundamental as the differences between the second and third estates. We can find the seeds of their conflicts growing out of our economy's transition from the simple fabrication methods of blacksmiths, carpenters and other medieval craftsmen to the large factories that marked the onset of the industrial revolution.

In the early years of the industrial revolution, with hundreds or even thousands of workers in a single factory, the balance of market control was tipped to the side of the second estate. The handful of employers were pretty much able to dictate wages and working conditions.

Workers had about the same status as felled trees, molten steel or railroad cars filled with slaughterhouse-bound cattle. Wages were extremely low and working conditions were, at best, downright deadly. That's when unions came on the scene.

Battles between the new unions and the fat cat employers often turned bloody. Companies didn't hesitate to use force—armed security guards and government soldiers—on the rabble-rousers. The unions fought back with an assortment of their own guerrilla tactics. Most of the violence ended with laws and court cases in the 1930s that forged a set of collective bargaining rules.

Let's try again with this brief excerpt from, "A National Care Agenda," by Suzanne Gordon, which appeared in the January 1991 edition of *The Atlantic Monthly*:

The United States is experiencing an extreme crisis in caring. As a society we cannot seem to muster the political will to care for the most precious things we produce: other human beings.

The United Sates has slipped to 25th place in the world in its infant-mortality rate. Twenty percent of America's children are destitute. More then 37 million people have no health insurance; 20 million to 30 million more are underinsured. Today, as patients are discharged earlier and earlier from the nation's hospitals, family members are increasingly asked to provide for their complex medical and emotional needs.

It is estimated that 1.8 million women care for children and elders simultaneously, and 33 percent of women do so in addition to holding down jobs.

Yet not only do these caregivers, who relieve our health-care system of a tremendous financial burden, receive little help; they are often penalized for providing such care, through the loss of wages or of the job itself.

The author is throwing around a lot of statistics to impress upon her readers that the United States must give some consideration to people who provide infants and older people with home health care. Should we remember the statistics about infant mortality, inadequate health insurance, the burdens on working women? Should these statistics appear in our notes?

If we read linearly, starting at the beginning and plodding along to the last word, we probably would be tempted to write down these numbers and what they mean in our notes. But, if we were to look ahead in the article (and glance at the subheads), we'd find that the author is actually making a case for investments in home care by the federal government and talking about where the money should come from.

Therefore, the statistics are not especially important, but the enormity of the problem to which they give credence *is*.

I didn't always keep my summaries to five words, but I distilled the main ideas to the fewest words I could.

Nor did I always write one summary statement per paragraph—just what was needed to capture the main idea or ideas from each paragraph.

Chapter 4

Gathering the facts

Now, what I want is Facts. Teach these boys and girls nothing but Facts. Facts alone are wanted in life. Plant nothing else, and root out everything else. You can only form the minds of reasoning animals upon Facts: Nothing else will ever be of any service to them. This is the principle on which I bring up my own children, and this is the principle on which I bring up these children. Stick to Facts, sir!

—Charles Dickens, *Hard Times*

Seeking out the facts, as Dickens's character would have us do, is also an effective way to confront your classroom reading assignments.

While such a "just the facts, ma'am" approach is not the whole formula for scholastic success, you'll find that the vast majority of your assigned reading requires a thorough recall of the facts.

In the previous chapter, we discussed the "forest"—the main idea. In this chapter, we will concentrate on "the trees"—how to read to gather facts, the specific details that support and develop the author's main point.

Facts: building blocks for ideas

Facts are the building blocks that give credibility to concepts and ideas. Your ability to gather and assimilate these facts will dramatically enhance your success at re-membering what the author wanted to communicate.

If, however, you spend so much time studying the trees that you lose sight of the forest, your reading effectiveness will be limited. You must learn to discern what facts are salient to your understanding, and which ones to leave for the next *Trivial Pursuit* update.

If you are trying to identify your purpose for reading this chapter, it's threefold:

1. To develop the skill of scanning a text for facts as quickly as possible.

2. To distinguish between an important detail and a trivial one.

3. To learn how to *skim* text—reading and absorbing its essence, even when you're not looking for anything in particular.

Deciphering the message

The author of any kind of writing should have some-thing to say, a message to communicate.

Unfortunately, such messages are often lost in the glut of verbiage many authors use to "dress up" their basic point. It's your job to rake through the mess and get to the heart of the text.

You need to approach each reading assignment with the mindset of Sherlock Holmes (or Joe Friday, if you prefer): There is a mystery to be solved, and you are the master detective. The goal is to figure out what the text is trying to communicate—regardless of how deeply it is buried in the quagmire of convoluted language.

What is the message?

The first step in any good investigation is to collect all of the clues. What are the facts? By spending a few minutes of your time discerning these concrete facts, you will be far better equipped to digest what it is the author is trying to communicate.

But how do you extract the facts when they appear to be hidden in an impenetrable forest of words? You may need a little help—from "who-what-when-where-why-and-how." It seems that the facts readily sally forth when these six trusty questions are called upon the scene.

Exercise: Read the following excerpt, keeping these six words in mind. After you have finished reading it, answer the questions that follow. Be careful—you may have to slow way down!

As Boris Yeltsin seeks to overcome an approval rating that hasn't reached double digits in months and confound countrymen who have declared he has no chance in the June elections, the Communists, sensing a chance for victory in a popular election, have suddenly become courteous and willing to compromise. Since they already dominate the newly-elected Parliament, their aim seems to be to keep the other political parties fighting among themselves, giving them little reason or excuse for establishing an anti-Communist coalition.

Gennadi Seleznyov, Speaker of the Parliament's lower house, or Duma, and a former editor of *Pravda*, looks more like a German banker than an old-style Communist Party apparatchik. That and his poise were two of the reasons he won out over former Central Committee member Valentin Kuptsov in the bid to become spokesperson for the "new and improved" Russian Communists, though the fight was prolonged and nasty.

And the new Speaker has his share of enemies, among them the ultra-nationalist Vladimir Zhirnovsky, who backed the candidate of the nationalist Our Home is Russia centrist party, Ivan Rybkin, in a bid to deny the powerful position to Seleznyov. While repeatedly calling for Yeltsin's resignation, Zhirnovsky has nevertheless supported the perhaps lame duck President on many fronts, including the invasion of Chechnya, the only party in Parliament to do so.

Luckily for Seleznyov, Grigory A. Yavlinsky, the liberal economist who leads Yablonko, the most reformist party in opposition to Yeltsin, refused to go along with Our Home is Russia and, by extension, Zhirnovsky. By withholding his votes, he assured Seleznyov's victory. While he maintained that he held out because he was anti-Communist, it was rumored that he had cut a deal for a couple of much-sought-after committee posts as the price of his votes.

All of this bitter infighting suggests that Seleznyov's gamble might just pay off—it is unlikely that an anti-Communist front will emerge in time for the elections. In addition, the results of the last election must leave him sanguine. Although his party won 149 votes, more than any other (Mr. Zhirinovsky's party was in second place, with 51), in reality the Communists are only a few votes shy of the 226 needed for an outright majority. It turns out that many of the 225 "independent" candidates who ran successfully were not as independent as they had declared—nearly one third of them can be counted on to support Seleznyov's programs.

Such control, unfortunately, tends to indicate that the new Duma will be far less flamboyant and much duller than the old, though undoubtedly more disciplined. Unlike the Speaker, many of the new Communist deputies *are* old-time apparatchiks who are quite accustomed to towing the party line and far less anxious to indulge in free speech.

1. The liberal economist who leads Yablonko is:

    A. Vladimir Zhirnovsky.

    B. Boris Yeltsin.

    C. Grigory A. Yavlinsky.

    D. Ivan Rybkin.

    E. Valentin Kuptsov.

2. Which of these ideas is *not* suggested in the passage?

    A. Vladimir Zhirnovsky is an ultra-nationalist.

    B. The Parliament's lower house is also known as the Duma.

    C. Ivan Rybkin was the candidate of the Our Home is Russia centrist party.

    D. Boris Yeltsin has had a high approval rating throughout the past few months.

    E. Yablonko is the most reformist party in opposition to Yeltsin.

3. How many votes are needed for an outright majority?

    A. 225.

    B. 226.

    C. 51.

    D. 149.

    E. None of the above.

4. The main purpose of this passage is to explain:

    A. The history of Communism.

    B. The lifestyle of Ivan Rybkin.

    C. The odds of the June election are in favor of the Communist party.

    D. The fight for the Speakership.

    E. The old and new Duma.

5. Using the context of the passage, how would "apparatchiks" be best described?

    A. Radical.

    B. Bold.

    C. Pioneering.

    D. Inexperienced.

    E. Traditional.

In the preceding exercise, you should have quickly read through the text and been able to answer all five questions. If it took you more than three minutes to do so, you spent too much time. You were reading *only* to answer our six questions—"who?", "what?", "when?", "where?", "why?" and "how?" Your purpose was to get to the facts, nothing more.

Scanning, skimming, reading, remembering

Most everyone I know confuses *skim* and *scan*. Let me set the record straight. *Skim is to read quickly and superficially. Scan is to read carefully but for a specific item.* So when you *skim* a reading selection, you are reading it in its entirety, though you're only hitting the "highlights."

When you *scan* a selection, you are reading it in detail but only until you find what you're looking for. Scanning is the technique we all employ when using the phone book—unless, of course, you're in the habit of reading every name in the book to find the one you're looking for. When you scan, your eyes do not look at every word, read every sentence or think about every paragraph. Instead, they rapidly move across the page to find just what you are looking for and then read that carefully.

Scanning is the *fastest* reading rate of all—although you are reading in detail, you are *not* seeking to comprehend or remember anything that you see until you find the bit of information you're looking for.

When I was in college, I would begin any assignment by reading the first sentence of every paragraph and trying to answer the questions at the chapter's end. If this did not give me a pretty good idea of the content and important details of that chapter, then—and only then—would I read it more thoroughly.

I'm sure this method of skimming for the facts saved me countless hours of time (and boredom).

Ask first, then look

When skimming for detail, you will often have a particular question, date or fact to find. You should approach the text much like the dictionary—knowing the word, you just skim the pages to find its definition. If you must answer a specific question or read about a historic figure, you simply find a source—book, magazine or encyclopedia—and quickly skim the text for the answer or person.

You probably are assigned a lot of reading that can be accomplished by skimming for facts. By establishing the questions you want answered *before* you begin to read, you can quickly browse through the material, extracting only the information you need.

Let's say you're reading a U.S. history text with the goal of identifying the key players in the Watergate Affair. You can breeze through the section that paints a picture of the day's political scene. You can whiz through the description of the Watergate Towers. And you can briefly skim the highlights of other questionable and clandestine political activity in the American past. You *know* what—or who—you're looking for. And there they are—Chuck Colson, John Dean, Mitchell, Liddy—the whole gang. Now you can start to *read.*

By identifying the questions you wanted to answer (*a.k.a.* your purpose) in advance, you would be able to skim the chapter and answer your questions in a lot less time than it would have taken to painstakingly read every word.

As a general rule, if you are reading textbook material word for word, you probably are wasting quite a bit of your study time. Good readers are able to discern what they should read in this manner and what they can afford to skim. When trying to simply gather detail and facts, skimming a text is a simple and very important shortcut.

Alternatively, our ability to skim a chapter—even something you need to read more critically—will enable you to develop a general sense of what the chapter is about and how thoroughly it needs to be read.

Exercise: Answer the following questions by skimming the paragraph that follows.

1. How many days are in an astronomical year?
2. Calendar years have how many days? Hours? Minutes? Seconds?
3. To regain the fraction of a day lost each calendar year, what is done?

Why do we have leap years? They occur to make up the day lost by the fact that our calendar year and the astronomical year do not coincide exactly. An astronomical year has 2,424 days. In calendar years, this is 365 days, five hours, 45 minutes, and 12 seconds. The extra fraction of a day is made up by what we call leap years—when we add an extra day to February. This is done to keep our calendar year in step with the seasons, which are based on the astronomical year.

If this were part of your assigned reading, you would be finished when you had answered the questions. "But I didn't read it," you protest. Can you write a one-sentence summary of the paragraph? If you *can*, and you answered the questions correctly, then you know all you need to.

Skimming, or prereading, is a valuable step even if you aren't seeking specific facts. When skimming for a general overview, there's a very simple procedure to follow:

1. If there is a title or heading, *rephrase it as a question.* This will be your purpose for reading.
2. Examine all the *subheadings, illustrations and graphics,* as these will help you identify the significant matter within the text.
3. Read thoroughly the *introductory paragraphs,* the summary and any questions at the chapter's end.

4. Read the *first sentence* of every paragraph. As we found in Chapter 3, this is generally where the main idea of a text is found.

5. *Evaluate* what you have gained from this process: Can you answer the questions at the end of the chapter? Could you intelligently participate in a class discussion of the material?

6. *Write* a brief summary that encapsulates what you have learned from your skimming.

7. Based on this evaluation, *decide* whether a more thorough reading is required.

Exercise: Let's see how well you can skim for an overview, rather than for specific facts. Read the following two passages, then follow the seven steps outlined above for each:

Five major scandals tainted the administration of President Ulysses S. Grant. Although the hero of Vicksburg was the first president to encounter charges of substantial wrongdoing during his administration, it was never proved that he was directly involved in any criminal acts nor that he profited from any of the acts of others.

The first incident occurred in 1869, the first year of his presidency. Known as Black Friday, it involved speculators James Fisk and Jay Gould and their attempt to corner the gold market. By involving Grant's brother-in-law, they hoped to prevent the government from "dumping" its gold onto the market, which would make it impossible for their scheme to succeed. Grant was not directly involved in Fisk's and Gould's machinations, but he certainly gave the appearance of complicity, allowing himself to be entertained lavishly and publicly on Fisk's yacht. However, when the pair's aggressive purchases of gold sent its price skyrocketing in a matter of days, Grant acted swiftly, ordering the Treasury Department to sell off $4 million in gold reserves. While this ended Fisk's and Gould's attempt, this step brought ruin to a number of individuals and businesses that were "riding the wave" of gold fever and resulted in a national economic shock not matched until the 1929 stock market crash.

The second major scandal involved the embezzlement of massive amounts of money by the Credit Mobilier holding company, which was involved with the construction of the Union Pacific railway. To avoid being discovered, the conspirators heavily bribed members of Congress and officials of the Republican Party, of which Grant was the nominal head. Although this scandal erupted during a heated reelection campaign against newspaper publisher Horace Greeley, Grant was evidently completely uninvolved and was reelected handily.

Two other scandals involved taxes and the officials appointed to collect them. One tax collector, John Sanborn, managed to keep nearly half of the delinquent taxes he collected, a total that exceeded $200,000. But that paled in comparison to the fraud discovered by Treasury Secretary Benjamin H. Bristow among liquor distillers and the officials charged with collecting taxes from them. Although Grant called for swift action against all the conspirators, his fervor flagged when his trusted personal secretary, Orville Babcock, was implicated in the scheme. Although Grant slowed the investigation, 110 conspirators were eventually found guilty.

In the final year of Grant's second term, evidence mounted that Secretary of War W.W. Belknap had been taking bribes from corrupt white traders at Indian trading posts. Since Grant had made much of his earlier attempts to institute a fair and non-abusive set of policies toward the Indians, the scandal was a personal embarrassment, though, again, Grant was in no way directly involved. Faced with certain impeachment, Belknap resigned.

Self-Fulfilling Prophesies and Other Scientific Marvels*

A combination of proper analytic skills and common sense is required for an executive to be effective. Call it the place where art and science meet. When you have the overly scientific, you find yourself in Dr. Frankenstein's laboratory, which I did one day at a large consumer products company in California.

The organization was looking at a decline in business caused by a combination of more aggressive competition and their own failure to launch some new products that their plan had heavily relied on. So the employees were going to bear the brunt of management's failure in these two areas. A senior management meeting was held to decide how best to downsize and to create several levels of contingency to react to various levels of revenue losses (and various degrees of shareholder ire). You see, it's simple to earn the big bucks: The management team was putting a hierarchy of firings in place to deal with a bad year, a horrible year and a disastrous year. Imagine what would've happened if this talent and time had been devoted to trying to *improve* the year.

A particularly officious young woman from staffing and planning was invited to the meeting to provide some of the details of implementing the phased reductions. As the session progressed, I became mesmerized by her high-tech language for what was, to me, a high-touch problem. When asked at what point the second level of discharges would begin, for example, she replied:

"Attrits from the prime round should have been in the outplace mode, offsite, if they were of grades 8 or higher. Other attrits would simply be gone. If profit levels for the second quarter fall below 85 percent of plan as determined by this group, I will initiate secondary attrits. Human resources will inform and escort on the same day, which we advise be a Friday, if possible. Tertiary attrits will occur if profit falls below 75 percent of plan. Tertiary attrits will receive no outplace assistance, unless they are supergrade."

What this all meant, I deciphered, was that the people being let go were being referred to as "attrits" (short for *attrition*). This helped dehumanize the situation significantly. We could have been discussing reducing inventory or equipment leases.

This was a case of all head, all science. It was a pragmatic approach using computerlike precision to remove people as though they were merely expense items on a balance sheet. The result was disastrous for morale and did not address the underlying cause of the company's marketplace problems.

*Excerpted from *Our Emperors Have No Clothes* by Alan Weiss (Career Press, 1995)

While it may not be evident at first, you'll soon see how *skimming* can save you a lot of reading time. Even if a more in-depth reading is necessary, you will find that by having gone through this process, you will have developed the kind of skeletal framework that will make your further reading faster, easier and more meaningful. And if all you need is "just the facts, ma'am," your ability to *scan* a selection, chapter or book will save you minutes, if not hours, every week.

Whether you're skimming or scanning, you will have equipped yourself with the ability to better digest what it is the author is trying to communicate.

Chapter 5

The challenge of technical texts

You've already learned a lot of ways to improve your reading. It's time to examine the unique challenges posed by highly technical texts. Physics, trigonometry, chemistry, calculus—you know, subjects that three-fourths of all students avoid like the plague. Even those students who manage to do well in such subjects wouldn't dare call them "Mickey Mouse" courses.

More than any other kind of reading, these subjects demand a logical, organized approach, a step-by-step reading method.

And they require a detection of the text's *organizational devices*.

Developing the skill to identify the basic sequence of the text will enable you to follow the progression of thought, a progression that is vital to your comprehension and retention.

Why? In most technical writing, each concept is a like a building block of understanding—if you don't understand a particular section or concept, you won't be able to understand the *next* section, either.

Most technical books are saturated with ideas, terms, formulas and theories. The chapters are dense with information, compressing a great wealth of ideas into a small space. They demand to be read very carefully.

In order to get as much as possible from such reading assignments, you can take advantage of some devices to make sense of the organization. Here are five basics to watch for:

1. Definitions and terms.
2. Examples.
3. Classifications and listings.
4. Use of contrast.
5. Cause-effect relationships.

As you read any text, but certainly a highly specialized one, identifying these devices will help you grasp the main idea, as well as any details that are essential to your thorough understanding of the material.

Definitions and terminology

In reading any specialized text, you must begin at the beginning—understanding the terms particular to that discipline. Familiar, everyday words have very precise definitions in technical writing.

What do I mean? Take the word *nice*. You may compliment your friend's new sweater, telling her it's *nice*, meaning attractive. You may find that the new chemistry teacher is *nice*, meaning he doesn't give too much homework. And when your friend uses the word *nice* to describe the blind date she's set up for you, it may mean something completely different—and insidious.

Everyday words can have a variety of meanings, some of them even contradictory, depending on the context in which they're used.

In contrast, in the sciences, terminology has fixed and specific meanings. For example, the definition of elasticity—*"the ability of a solid to regain its shape after a deforming force has been applied"*—is the same in Bangkok or Brooklyn. Such exact terminology enables scientists to communicate with the precision their discipline requires.

Definitions may vary in length. One term may require a one-sentence definition, others merit entire paragraphs. Some may even need a whole chapter to accurately communicate the definition.

Examples help clarify the abstract

A second communication tool is the example. Authors use examples to bridge abstract principles to concrete illustrations. These examples are essential to your ability to comprehend intricate and complicated theories.

Unlike other writing, technical writing places a very high premium on brevity. Economizing words is the key to covering a large volume of knowledge in a relatively small space. Few technical texts or articles include anecdotal matter or chatty stories of the author's experience.

This fact challenges the reader to pay particular attention to the examples that are included. Why? Technical writing often is filled with new or foreign ideas—many of which are not readily digestible. They are difficult in part because they are abstract. Examples work to clarify these concepts, hopefully in terms more easily understood.

For example, it may be difficult for you to make sense of the definition of symbiosis—*"the living together of two dissimilar organisms, especially when mutually beneficial"*—but the example of the bird that picks food from the crocodile's teeth, thereby feeding itself and keeping the crocodile cavity-free, helps bring it home.

Classification and listings

A third tool frequently utilized in texts is classification and listings. Classifying is the process by which common subjects are categorized under a general heading.

Some examples:

> *Matter may occur in three forms: solid, liquid or gas.*

Classification: Three forms of matter
Listing: Solid, liquid, gas

> *The social sciences are psychology, economics and sociology.*

Classification: Social sciences
Listing: Psychology, economics, sociology

Especially in technical writing, authors use classification to categorize extensive lists of detail. Such writings may have several categories and subcategories that organize these details into some manageable fashion.

Comparing/contrasting

A fourth tool used in communicating difficult information is that of comparing and contrasting. Texts use this tool to bring complicated material into focus by offering a similar or opposing picture.

Such devices are invaluable in grasping concepts that do not conjure a picture in your mind. Gravity, for example, is not something that can be readily pictured—it's not a tangible object that can be described.

Through comparison, a text relates a concept to one that has been previously defined—or to one a reader may readily understand. Through contrast, the text concentrates on the differences and distinctions between two ideas. By focusing on distinguishing features, these ideas become clearer as one idea is held up against another.

Cause-effect relationships

A final tool that texts employ to communicate is the cause-effect relationship. This device is best defined in the context of science, where it is the fundamental quest of most scientific research.

Science begins with the observation of the effect—what is happening?

It is snowing.

The next step is to conduct research into the cause: *Why* is it snowing? Detailing this cause-effect relationship is often the essence of scientific and technical writing.

Cause-effect relationships may be written in many ways. The effect may be stated first, followed by the cause. An effect may be the result of several connected causes—a causal chain. And a cause may have numerous effects.

In your reading, it is vital that you recognize this relationship and its significance.

Read with a plan

More than any other type of writing, highly specialized, technical writing must be read with a plan. You can't approach your reading assignment merely with the goal of completing it. Such mindless reading will leave you confused and frustrated, drowning in an ocean of theory, concepts, terms and examples.

Your plan should incorporate the following guidelines:

1. **Learn the terms** that are essential to understanding the concepts presented. Knowing the precise definitions that the author uses will enable you to follow his chain of thought through the text.

2. **Determine the structure or organization of the text.** Most chapters have a definite pattern that forms the skeleton of the material. A book may begin with a statement of a theory, give examples, provide sample problems, then summarize. Often this pattern can be discerned through a preview of the table of contents or the titles and subtitles.

3. **Skim the chapter** to get a sense of the author's viewpoint. Ask questions to define your purpose in reading. Use any summaries or review questions to guide your reading.

4. **Do a thorough analytical reading** of the text. Do not proceed from one section to the next until you have a clear understanding of the section you are reading—the concepts generally build upon each other. To proceed to a new section without understanding the ones that precede it is, at best, futile.

5. **Immediately upon concluding your thorough reading, review!** Write a summary of the concepts and theories you need to remember. Answer any questions raised when you skimmed the text. Do the problems. If possible, apply the formulas.

Improve Your Reading

Technical material is saturated with ideas. When reading it, you must be convinced of one fact: Every individual word counts! You will want to read such material with the utmost concentration—it is not meant to be sped through.

Good readers know that such material demands a slow read that concentrates on achieving the greatest level of retention.

- Every definition has to be digested.

- Every formula must be committed to memory.

- Every example needs to be considered.

To improve your reading of such technical material you will want to hone the skill of identifying the devices an author uses to communicate. In so doing, you will be able to connect the chain of thought that occurs. When reading such texts—or attempting to work out technical problems— try the following "tricks":

- Whenever you can, "translate" formulas and numbers into words. To test your understanding, try to put your translation into *different* words.

- Even if you're not particularly visual, pictures can often help. You should try translating a particularly vexing math problem into a drawing or diagram.

- Before you even get down to solving a problem, is there any way for you to estimate the answer or, at least, to estimate the range within which the answer should fall (greater than one, but less than 10)? This is the easy way to at least make sure you wind up in the right ballpark.

- Play around. There are often different paths to the same solution, or even equally valid solutions. If you find one, try to find others. This is a great way to increase your understanding of all the principles involved.

- When you are checking your calculations, try working *backwards*. I've found it an easier way to catch simple mathematical errors.

- Try to figure out what is being asked, what principles are involved, what information is important and what is not.

- Teach someone else. Trying to explain mathematical concepts to someone else will quickly pinpoint what you really know or don't know. It's virtually impossible to get someone else—especially someone who is slower than you at all this stuff—to understand if you don't!

Chapter 6

Becoming a critical reader

After four years of undergraduate work, before my dear alma mater would award me the degree for which I felt my dollars, sweat and blood had amply paid, I was made to endure a six-hour essay test. We literature majors were given one question—"Analyze and interpret the following:" (the "following" being a poem we had never seen before...and several blue books in which to write our erudite answers).

Unbelievable?

Hardly!

This test was given in much the same way that the Educational Testing Service gives their PSAT, SAT, ACT, LSAT and GMAT verbal tests. In the notorious reading comprehension section, you are required to read a distilled passage—which, unless you've stolen a peek at the exam, you have never seen—and then given four to six questions to determine if you have any clue as to what you just read.

You will find that there are many times, particularly in comparative literature classes, when you will need to read something with great care in order to remember details and interpret meaning. Hester Prynne's red monogram, Poe's talking raven and Samuel Beckett's mysterious friend all require a little more analysis than a superficial interpretation of props and plot.

Yet such detailed, analytical reading is not limited to literature. Political dissertations, historical analysis and even scientific research may require more careful reading than the latest "space opera."

Such reading is often referred to as *critical reading,* a type of reading during which you seek to distinguish thoughts, ideas or concepts—each demanding thorough study and evaluation.

Critical reading requires that you are able to identify the author's arguments, measure their worth and truth and apply what is pertinent to your own experience. Unlike skimming, critical reading challenges the reader to concentrate at the highest level possible.

Prepare yourself to read critically

When preparing to read critically, you must lay the groundwork for concentration. Just as an athlete must ready himself mentally to achieve peak performance, you will want to ready yourself before you begin to read.

To prepare to read critically:

1. You must have a clearly defined purpose for reading. Make sure that you've identified your purpose before you begin.
2. Pay attention! Avoid letting your mind wander to that conversation you and your friend had today at lunch. Minimize distractions and interruptions—anything or anyone that causes you to break your focus.

3. Find your optimum study environment—a quiet corner in the library, your own room, wherever. In absolute silence, or with your new CD playing. (Be sure to read **Manage Your Time** or **Get Organized**, two of the nine books in my **How to Study Program**, for more tips on finding *your* perfect study environment.)

4. Do not concern yourself with how fast or slowly you read. Your goal should be to understand the material, not to find out how fast you can get it over with.

5. If it seems that you will need several hours to complete your reading, you might break the longer assignments into smaller, more manageable parts, then reward yourself at the end of each of these sections by taking brief breaks.

If you take these steps prior to reading any text that requires your utmost concentration, you will find that your mind is readied for the kind of focus necessary to read critically. Make a *habit* of such preparations and you will set yourself up to succeed.

Prereading is a must

Once you have prepared your mind to read, the next step is to understand the big picture—what is the author's thesis or main idea? Good comprehension is the consequence of your ability to grasp the main point of what the author is trying to communicate.

And grasping this message is accomplished through skimming the text, as we discussed in Chapter 4. Let's review the basic steps:

1. If there is a title or heading, rephrase it as a question. This will support your purpose for reading.
2. Examine all subheadings, illustrations and graphics, as these will help you identify the significant matter within the text.
3. Read the introductory paragraphs, summary and any questions at the end of the chapter.
4. Read the first sentence of every paragraph. In Chapter 3 you learned that this is generally where the main idea is found.
5. Evaluate what you have gained from this process: Can you answer the questions at the chapter's end? Could you intelligently participate in a class discussion of the material?
6. Write a brief summary of what you have learned from your skimming.

By beginning critical reading with a 20-minute skim of the text, you should be ready to answer three questions:

1. What is the text's principal message or viewpoint?
2. Is an obvious chain of thought or reasoning revealed?
3. What major points are addressed?

Now, read it

Once you identify and understand the basic skeleton of the material, your actual "read" of the material—following the details, reasoning and chain of thought—is simply a matter of attaching meat to the bones.

This digestive process involves learning to interpret and evaluate what is written, what is directly stated and what can be inferred from the context.

Effective analytical reading requires that you, the reader, distinguish the explicit, literal meaning of words *(denotation)* and what suggestions or intentions are intimated by the general content *(connotation)*.

Analyzing: what the words connote

Words and writing have two levels of meaning that are important to the reader's comprehension.

The first level is the literal or descriptive meaning. What a word expressly *denotes* means the specific, precise definition you'd find in *Webster*.

Connotation involves this second level of meaning— that which incorporates the total *significance* of the words.

What does that mean? Beyond a literal definition, words communicate emotion, bias, attitude and perspective. Analyzing any text involves learning to interpret what is implied, just as much as what is expressly stated.

15 questions to help you

Beyond grasping the meaning of words and phrases, critical reading requires that you ask questions. Here are 15 questions that will help you effectively analyze and interpret most of what you read.

1. Is there a clear message communicated throughout?
2. Are the relationships between the points direct and clear?
3. Is there a relationship between your experience and the author's?
4. Are the details factual?

5. Are the examples and evidence relevant?
6. Is there consistency of thought?
7. What is the author's bias or slant?
8. What is the author's motive?
9. What does the author want you to believe?
10. Does this jibe with your own beliefs or experiences?
11. Is the author rational or subjective?
12. Is there a confusion between feelings and facts?
13. Are the main points logically ordered?
14. Are the arguments and conclusions consistent?
15. Are the explanations clear?

Obviously, this list of questions is not all-inclusive, but it will give you a jump start when critical reading is required. Remember, the essential ingredient to any effective analysis and interpretation is the questions you ask.

Summarizing: the final step

Nothing will be more important to your recall than learning to condense what you read into a clear and concise summary.

Many of you have learned to do this by excerpting entire segments or sentences from a text, certainly not a very efficient method for summarizing.

I recommend using the traditional outline (which is explained in detail in my book, *Take Notes*).

Another suggestion is to use a two-step process called *diagramming,* which calls for the reader to *diagram* or illustrate the content he's just read, then write a brief synopsis of what he's learned.

Similar to outlining, diagramming helps the reader to visualize the relationships between various thoughts and ideas. Concept diagrams, or concept trees, are very useful visual aids for depicting the structure of a textbook.

Unless you have a photographic memory, you will find that recalling a picture of the main points will greatly increase what you remember. Beyond this, such diagrams require that you distill what is essential to the text and how it relates to the main message.

Suppose you read a chapter in your biology assignment about the parts of a cell. Your diagram might reduce your reading material to look like the following:

Parts of a Cell

Outside of Cell	**Inside of Cell**
cell wall	cytoplasm
cell membrane	vacuoles
nucleus chloroplasts	chlorophyll

More than a listing of main points, a diagram allows you to picture how parts fit together, which enhances your ability to recall the information you've read. This is especially true the more "visual" you are.

Distill it into a synopsis

The second step in the process of summarizing is to write a brief synopsis of what you've learned. When you need to review the material, diagrams will remind you of the significant elements in the text. Your synopsis will remind you of the main idea.

The goal here is to put in your own words what you gleaned from what you read. You will find this process an invaluable gauge of whether you have understood the message—and on what level.

Use this method one chapter at a time, and do not proceed to the *next* chapter until you have completed the following exercise:

1. Write definitions of any key terms you feel are essential to understanding the topic.

2. Write questions and answers you feel clarify the topic.

3. Write any questions for which you don't have answers—then make sure you find them through rereading, further research or asking another student or your teacher.

4. Even if you still have unanswered questions, move on to the next section and complete numbers one to three for that section. (And so on, until your reading assignment is complete.) See if this method doesn't help you get a better handle on any assignment right from the start.

Critical reading is not easy. It requires a lot more concentration and effort than the quick-reference reading that you can get away with for much of your day-to-day class assignments. And I won't kid you—much of the reading you'll do in the latter years of high school and throughout college will be critical reading.

But if you follow the steps I've outlined for each critical reading assignment that you tackle—preparing yourself for the read, doing a preread skim, followed by an analytical reading, concluding with a summarization—you'll discover that critical reading can be a much smoother, even rewarding, experience!

The method you probably learned

If you were taught a specific reading method in school, it was probably the one developed back in the 1940s that is abbreviated "SQ3R." This stands for Survey, Question, Read, Recite and Review. Here's how the process works:

Survey. Preread the chapter, concentrating on topic sentences, subheads and review questions, in order to get an overview of what's ahead.

Question. Once you've surveyed the chapter, ask yourself what information is contained in it. Consider turning the subheads into questions as an exercise.

Read. Now read the first section thoroughly, attempting to answer the questions you've posed. Take notes, highlight, underline, map.

Recite. Now answer the questions *without* looking at your notes or the text. When you're done, go on to the next section. Continue this detailed reading/reciting tandem until you finish the chapter (or the assignment).

Review. Go back over the entire assignment.

Does this sound familiar? I agree. I think this method is completely incorporated into the steps I've outlined in this and previous chapters, so I left it out of a previous edition of this book. Since some teachers have taken me to task for failing to mention it, here it is.

Frankly, I think the detailed method I've proposed—and the helpful advice along the way—covers far more ground.

Chapter 7

Reading the literature

"Will you walk a little faster?" said a whiting to a snail.

"There's a porpoise close behind us and he's treading on my tail!"

"If I'd been the whiting," said Alice, whose thoughts were still running on the song, "I'd have said to the porpoise, 'Keep back, please; we don't want you with us!'"

"They were obliged to have him with them," the Mock Turtle said. "No wise fish would go anywhere without a Porpoise."

"Wouldn't it really?" said Alice in a tone of great surprise.

"Of course not," said the Mock Turtle. "Why, if a fish came to me, and told me he was going on a journey, I should say, 'With what porpoise?'"

"Don't you mean 'purpose?'" said Alice.

"I mean what I say," the Mock Turtle replied in an offended tone.

—Lewis Carroll, *Alice in Wonderland*

In this excerpt, you could enjoy the nonsensical picture of a porpoise pushing a snail and whiting to walk faster. You might laugh at the confusion of "porpoise" and "purpose" by the Mock Turtle. Or you could discern the *message*—that you need to have a purpose when you are on a journey...or reading.

In today's world of Sega, Mortal Kombat and Green Day, literature often takes a back seat. So much so that many of your classmates (not *you*, of course) may not even know that *Alice in Wonderland* is an important piece of literature.

Why should you care about literature? Who needs to read the book when you can see the movie?

While I didn't write this book to give you a lecture on the merits of the classics, please bear with me for a couple of paragraphs.

The greatest involvement device

Unlike anything else, literature *involves* the reader in the story. How? There are no joysticks to manipulate, no "sensurround" sound to engulf you. Your imagination is your only involvement device, but it far surpasses any high-tech computer gimmicks.

Your imagination makes reading the ultimate adventure. It allows you to immerse yourself in the story—identifying with the protagonist, fighting his battles, experiencing his fears, sharing his victories. You may become so involved, you end up staying up well past your bedtime, turning page after page late into the night!

Your imagination is the vehicle that allows you to explore a million different lives, from floating down the Mississippi River on a raft, to suffering through a star-crossed love affair, to having tea with the March Hare and the Mad Hatter, as our Alice did.

Creative writing may be serious or humorous or sub-lime...or all three. It is often subtle; meanings are elusive and delicate. Such writing, when done effectively, evokes emotional responses. You get angry. You shed a tear. You chuckle. An author's expression strikes a chord that moves you. You and the author communicate on a level that is far beyond an exchange of facts and information.

Enough said. Assuming that I have converted all you literature skeptics to avid library loiterers (and even if I haven't), I'll offer some advice to help you begin your journey to literary appreciation. It begins with understanding the basic roadmap.

Which reading method? Pleasure or critical?

While I certainly encourage you to approach your reading with the enthusiasm and anticipation that would justify the pleasure-reading method (see Chapter 2), the demands of your teacher who assigns the reading will probably require the *critical* reading method.

Reading literature requires most of the skills we've discussed previously.

There are devices and clues to ferret out that will help you follow the story and understand its meaning better.

You will analyze and interpret what the author is saying and evaluate its worth.

But in addition, in literature, you will be able to appreciate the *words* themselves. In textbooks, you often must penetrate a thick jungle of tangled sentences and murky paragraphs to find the information you seek.

Great literature *is* its language. It's the flow and ebb of its words, the cadence of its sentences, as much as it is story and theme.

As you read more, you'll uncover the diversity of tapestries that different authors weave with words. You may discover similar themes coursing through the works of authors like Ernest Hemingway or Thomas Hardy, but their use of language is as different as desert and forest. The composition of the words themselves is an element you'll want to examine as you critically read literature.

Fiction: just another word for storytelling

Most fiction is an attempt to tell a story. There is a *beginning,* in which the characters and the setting are introduced. There is a *conflict or struggle* (middle) that advances the story to a *climax* (end)—where the conflict is resolved. A final *denouement* or "winding up" clarifies the conclusion of the story.

Your literature class will address all of these parts using literary terms that are often more confusing than helpful. The following are brief definitions of some of the more important ones:

Plot. The order or sequence of the story—how it proceeds from the opening through the climax. Your ability to understand and appreciate literature depends upon how well you follow the plot—the *story*.

Characterization. The personalities or characters central to the story—the heroes, heroines and villains. You will want to identify the main characters of the story and their relationship to the struggle or conflict. Pay particular attention as to whether the characters are three dimensional—are they real and believable?

Theme. The controlling message or subject of the story; the moral or idea that the author is using the plot and characters to communicate. Some examples: man's inhumanity to man, man's impotency in his environment, the corrupting influence of power, greed and unrequited love. Just as with nonfiction, you need to discern this theme to really understand what it is the author wants to communicate.

Setting. The time and place in which the story takes place. This is especially important when reading a historical novel or one that takes you to another culture.

Point of view. Who is telling the story? Is it one of the central characters giving you flashbacks or a first-person perspective? Or is it a third-person narrator offering commentary and observations on the characters, the setting and the plot? This person moves the story along and gives it an overall tone.

The first step in reading literature is to familiarize yourself with these concepts and then try to recognize them in each novel or short story you read.

The second step is the same as for reading nonfiction— to identify your purpose for reading.

Allow your purpose to define how you will read. If you are reading to be entertained, then a pleasure read is the way to go. If you're reading for a class and will be required to participate in discussions or be tested on the material, you'll want to do a critical read.

How long should it take?

As a general rule, fiction is not meant to be read over a period of months—or even weeks. Try to read it as quickly as possible to get a full appreciation of the author's plot, character and theme. You should read fast enough to progress through the plot, get a sense of the characters and their struggles and hear the author's message or theme.

It's helpful to set a goal as to when you want to finish your reading. Frequently, of course, this will already be set for you, if your reading is a class assignment.

You should, however, set daily goals. Set aside one or two hours to read, or set a goal of reading three chapters a day until you finish. Reading sporadically—10 minutes one day, a half hour the next, then not picking up the book until several days later—means that you'll lose track of the plot and characters and just as quickly lose interest.

Too often when students do not establish a regular schedule, their reading becomes fragmented, making it very difficult to piece together the whole story. A reasonable goal is to try to read a novel in less than a week, a short story in one sitting. To achieve this goal, once you begin, you should read every day until you finish. By doing this, the story and characters will stay fresh in your mind.

If you try to read fiction more rapidly, you will greatly increase your enjoyment of it. It is vitally important that as you try to read faster, you give the story your full attention. By doing this you will be surprised by how improved your understanding and appreciation are.

To speed your reading of fiction, try this experiment:

1. Find a novel or short story that interests you and is relatively easy to read. Tomes like *Ulysses or The Naked Lunch* shouldn't be candidates.

2. Set aside two or three hours to invest in reading the book. If at all possible, finish it in one sitting. If you can't, then allocate the same amount of time each day until you do.

By trying this experiment, you will discover that fiction is *intended* to be read this way—whenever possible, in one sitting. It is as if you are sitting at a master storyteller's feet as he spins his tale. You want to know how the story ends and what happens to the hero.

Will the villain get his comeuppance? Will the hero get the girl? Or ride off with his horse?

You'll find that you appreciate the story far more at the end than anywhere in the middle.

Some other tips for reading fiction:

1. Understand the plot and maintain awareness of its progression.

2. Take breaks to review what has occurred and who is involved.

3. Vary your reading method—from skimming transitional bridge material to carefully reading description and narration.

4. Question the story's theme. What is the message?

You're allowed to enjoy it

A final recommendation: Give yourself permission to *enjoy* what you are reading. You will be amazed at the difference this will make. Fiction, unlike any other reading, can take you on an adventure. Through your mind, you can journey to faraway lands, pretend you are someone else, feel emotions you may never otherwise experience. All this happens as you gain an appreciation of literature—as you learn to understand fiction and allow yourself to enjoy great stories.

Chapter 8

Focusing your mind

Concentration: It's one of the biggest challenges facing any reader.

Why? Unlike other activities, reading requires an *active* mind and a *passive* body. A deadly combination, especially when you've spent the day in classes and haven't had a chance to burn off that excess energy with a tennis match, a game of "hoops" or a quick run around campus.

Concentration-wise, reading can be more demanding than class lectures, homework assignments or note-taking. In class, you at least have vocal variety and the threat of being called on to keep you focused. And writing, while a sedentary activity, still requires some hand-eye coordination to keep your brain working.

Keep your mind on one thing

Concentration begins with the ability to keep your mind focused on one thing—your reading assignment. This is not an innate talent, but a learned discipline. Much like an athlete must learn to be so focused that she is completely unaffected by the screaming crowds, a good reader absorbs himself in what he's reading.

How does *your* mind discipline "rate"? Answer these questions to find out:

1. When I read, do I often allow random thoughts to steal my focus?

2. As I read, am I easily distracted by noises or other activities?

3. Am I watching the clock to see how long I have been reading?

There is no simple, magic formula for conjuring up concentration—especially when you're faced with a critical reading assignment you're not particularly looking forward to. But if you follow the preparatory steps I've discussed in previous chapters—define your purpose, skim for a preread, identify questions for which you will seek answers—you should find it a bit easier to stay focused.

Steps to better concentration

Here are some other practical steps I recommend to increase your ability to concentrate:

1. **Get some exercise** before you begin your reading. A game of racquetball, an exercise class, a workout at the gym, even a brisk walk, will help burn off *physical* energy so you'll be able to direct all of your *mental* energy to your reading.

2. **Read in the right place.** No, it's not in front of the TV, nor in your room if your roommate is hosting a pizza party. Reading is a solitary activity. Find a quiet corner, preferably in a place designated for study only—at your desk, in the library. Although tempting, reading on your bed can be dangerous if you're struggling to concentrate. You just may lose the battle and find yourself in the perfect place to doze off.

3. **Eliminate distractions.** If you've properly scheduled your reading time (see *Manage Your Time*), you won't be distracted by other pending assignments. If you're trying to read one assignment while worrying about another, your concentration—and comprehension—will inevitably suffer.

   Make sure there's nothing else in sight to vie for your attention. Are there letters on your desk that you need to respond to? Put them away and schedule some time to write back. Sirens and screams from the TV show in the other room? Turn it off, down or close your door.

4. **Plan breaks.** If you have three hours or more of reading ahead of you, the mere thought of it may be so discouraging that you'll lose your concentration before you even pick up the book. Schedule short 10- or 15-minute breaks after each hour of reading. Get up. Listen to some music. Stretch. If you must break more frequently, keep your breaks shorter. By breaking up your reading into smaller, more digestible bites, you'll be able to concentrate more effectively.

Wait! Don't start reading yet.

Have you defined your purpose for reading? Once again, you must have a clearly defined purpose or goal. What are you reading for? (We have addressed this numerous times, but spaced repetition is a very effective way to make a point.)

The point is that reading without purpose is the greatest means to getting nowhere, which is where you'll find your mind after about a half-hour.

Know why you are reading. If your teacher or professor has given you questions to answer, then you know what you're looking for. If not, ask your *own* questions, using the clues in your book (as discussed in Chapter 2).

An effective preread of the material should help you define your purpose and stimulate some interest in finding out more—which will result in increased concentration.

Motivation: crucial to concentration

Motivation is key to your success in just about any endeavor, whether it's graduating with honors, maintaining an effective time-management program or improving your reading. You can utilize all the tricks and steps I've mentioned in this chapter, but if you lack the motivation to read, you'll still find it a struggle to concentrate on your assignments.

There are two types of motivation—intrinsic and extrinsic. What's the difference?

An avid murder mystery fan, you buy stacks of paperbacks at the used bookstore and spend your free time with your nose buried in them. You love the challenge of figuring out "who did it" before you reach the end. In fact, you'd spend all weekend reading mysteries if you didn't have to complete a reading assignment for your political science class. You're not particularly interested in poli-sci, but your efforts on this assignment could secure you an A for the term, so you're determined to read the material and "ace" the exam.

Your motivation for reading the mysteries is intrinsic—you do it because you enjoy it. You don't get any awards. You don't get paid for it.

The poli-sci reading, on the other hand, requires external motivation. You're reading it because you want to earn a high grade in class. Your reward is external—beyond the reading itself.

Whether you are intrinsically motivated to read or doing it for some external reward doesn't matter as much as the fact that you are motivated by something! If you find it difficult to get excited about reading your economics assignment, remind yourself of how this exercise will help your grade—get yourself externally motivated.

If *that* doesn't get you motivated enough to read for three hours, there's nothing wrong with a little bribery. Reward yourself with something more immediate. Promise yourself that if you stay focused on your reading until it's completed, you can watch that video afterward. Or you can buy that new CD. (Be careful, though. If you need *lots* of extrinsic motivation, you could run out of money!)

The value of concentration can be summed up in one statement: Concentration is essential to comprehension. Where there is failure to focus, there will be little or no understanding.

Without concentration, you will see only words on a page.

Chapter 9

Retaining the information

The ultimate test of your comprehension is what you remember *after* you have finished your reading—what you walk away with.

As a student, most of your reading will be for classes in which, sooner or later, you'll be required to regurgitate the information you've read in some type of format—essay test, term paper, multiple-choice, true-false or fill-in-the-blank final.

So, beyond just being able to *complete* your reading assignments, you want to be sure you *remember* what you read.

All of you have probably had the experience of forgetting that important fact that made the difference between an A- and a B+ (or a B- and a C+). It was sitting right there, on the tip of your brain. But you couldn't quite remember it.

Memory can be improved

You probably know people with photographic (or near-photographic) memories. They know all the words to all the songs in *Rolling Stone's* Top Fifty, remind you of things you said to them three years ago and never forget anyone's birthday (or anniversary or "day we met" or "first kiss day," *ad infinitum*).

While some people seem to be able to retain information naturally, a good memory—like good concentration—*can* be learned. You can control what stays in your mind and what is forgotten. The key to this control is to learn and tap into the essential elements of good memory.

Some people remember with relative ease and have no problem retaining large volumes of information. Others often are aggravated by a faulty memory that seems to lose more than it retains. Several factors contribute to your capability to recall information you take in:

Intelligence, age and experience all play a role in how well you remember. Not everyone remembers the same way. You need to identify how these factors affect your memory and learn to maximize your strengths.

Laying a strong foundation is important to good memory. Most learning is an addition to something you already know. If you never grasped basic chemistry, then mastering organic chemistry will be virtually impossible. By developing a broad base of basic knowledge, you will enhance your ability to recall new information.

Motivation is key to improving your memory. A friend of mine, the consummate baseball fan, seems to know every baseball statistic from the beginning of time. He can spout off batting averages and ERAs from any decade for virtually any player, his favorite team's season schedule...and most of the other teams', too! While I wouldn't say he is the most intelligent guy I've ever met, he obviously loves baseball and is highly motivated to memorize as much as possible about his favorite subject.

You probably have a pet interest, too. Whether it's movies, music or sports, you've filled your brain with a mountain of information. Now, if you can learn that much about one subject, you are obviously capable of retaining information about other subjects—even chemistry. You just have to learn how to motivate yourself.

A method, system or process for retaining information is crucial to increasing your recall. This may include organizing your thinking, good study habits or mnemonic devices—some means that you utilize when you have to remember.

Using what you learn, soon after you learn it, is important to recall. It's fine to memorize a vocabulary list for a quick quiz, but if you wish to retain information for the long haul, you must reinforce your learning by using this knowledge. For example, you will add a new word to your permanent vocabulary if you make a point to use it, correctly, in a conversation.

The study of foreign languages, for many, proves frustrating when there are no opportunities outside of class to practice speaking the language. That's why foreign-language students often join conversation groups or study abroad—to reinforce retention of what they have learned by using it.

Why we forget

As you think about the elements of developing good memory, you can use them to address why you *forget*. The root of poor memory is usually found in one of these areas:

1. We fail to make the material meaningful.
2. We did not learn prerequisite material.
3. We fail to grasp what is to be remembered.
4. We do not have the desire to remember.
5. We allow apathy or boredom to dictate how we learn.
6. We have no set habit for learning.
7. We are disorganized and inefficient in our use of study time.
8. We do not use the knowledge we have gained.

All of us are inundated with information every day, bombarded with facts, concepts and opinion. We are capable of absorbing some information simply because the media drench us with it. (I've never read Nancy Reagan's notorious unauthorized biography, nor do I intend to, but how could I not be aware of her reputation for recycling Christmas gifts?)

In order to retain most information, we have to make a concerted effort to do so. We must make this same effort with the material we read.

How to remember

There are some basic tools that will help you remember what you read:

Understanding. You will remember only what you understand. When you read something and grasp the message, you have begun the process of retention. The way to test this is to state the message in your own words. Can you summarize the main idea? Unless you understand what is being said, you won't be able to decide whether it is to be remembered or discarded.

Desire. Let me repeat: You remember what you *choose* to remember. If you do not want to retain some piece of information or don't believe you *can,* then you *won't*! To remember the material, you must *want* to remember it and be convinced that you *will* remember it.

Overlearn. To insure that you retain material, you need to go beyond simply doing the assignment. To really remember what you learn, you should learn material thoroughly, or *over*learn. This involves prereading the text, doing a critical read and having some definite means of review that reinforces what you should have learned.

Systematize. It's more difficult to remember random thoughts or numbers than those organized in some pattern. For example, which phone number is easier to remember: 538-6284 or 678-1234? Once you recognize the pattern in the second number, it takes much less effort to remember than the first. You should develop the ability to discern the structure that exists and recall it when you try to remember. Have a system to help you recall how information is organized and connected.

Association. It's helpful to attach or associate what you are trying to recall to something you already have in your memory. Mentally link new material to existing knowledge so that you are giving this new thought some context in your mind.

If we take these principles and apply them to your reading assignment, we can develop a procedure that will increase what you take with you from your reading.

A procedure to improve recall

Each time you attempt to read something that you must recall, use this six-step process:

1. **Evaluate the material and define your purpose** for reading. Identify your interest level and get a sense of how difficult the material is.

2. **Choose appropriate reading techniques** for the purpose of your reading. If you are reading to grasp the main idea then that is what you will recall.

3. **Identify the important facts.** Remember what you need to. Identify associations that connect the details you must recall.

4. **Take notes.** Use your own words to give a synopsis of the main ideas. Use an outline, diagram or concept tree to show relationship and pattern. Your notes provide an important backup to your memory. Writing down key points will further reinforce your ability to remember.

5. **Review.** Quiz yourself on those things you must remember. Develop some system by which you review notes at least three times before you are required to recall. The first review should be shortly after you've read, the second should come a few days later and the final should take place just before you are expected to recall. This process will help you avoid cram sessions.

6. **Implement.** Find opportunities to *use* the knowledge you have gained. Study groups and class discussions are invaluable opportunities to implement what you've learned.

Memorizing and mnemonics

To this point, we have concentrated on the fundamentals of remembering and retention. There are some specific methods to help you recall when you must remember a lot of specific facts. The first of these is memorization—the process of trying to recall information word-for-word.

Memorize only when you are required to remember something for a relatively short time—when you have a history quiz on battle dates, a chemistry test on specific formulas or a vocabulary test in French.

When memorization is required, you should do whatever is necessary to impress the exact information on your mind. Repetition is probably the most effective method. Write down the information on a 3 x 5 card and use it as a flashcard. You must quiz yourself frequently to assure that you know the information perfectly.

A second technique for recalling lots of details is *mnemonics*. A mnemonic device is used to help recall large bits of information which may or may not be logically connected. Such mnemonics are invaluable when you must remember facts not arranged in a clear fashion, items that are quite complicated and numerous items that are a part of a series.

One of the simplest methods is to try to remember just the first letter of a sequence. That's how Roy G. Biv (the colors of the spectrum, in order from left to right—red, orange, yellow, green, blue, indigo, violet) came about. Or **E**very **G**ood **B**oy **D**oes **F**ine, to remember the notes on the musical staff. Or, perhaps the simplest of all, **FACE**, to remember the notes in between. (The latter two work opposite of old Roy—using *words* to remember *letters*.) Of course, not many sequences work out so nicely. If you tried to memorize the signs of the zodiac with this method, you'd wind up with **A**ries, **T**aurus, **G**emini, **C**ancer, **L**eo, **V**irgo, **L**ibra, **S**corpio, **S**agittarius, **C**apricorn, **A**quarius, **P**isces. Now many of you can make a name or a place or something out of ATGCLVLSSCAP, but I can't!

One solution is to make up a simple sentence that uses the first letters of the list you're trying to remember as the first letters of each word. For example, **A** **T**all **G**iraffe **C**hewed **L**eaves **V**ery **L**ow, **S**ome **S**low **C**ows **A**t **P**lay.

Wait a minute! It's the same number of words. Why not just figure out some way to memorize the first set of words? What's better about the second set? A couple of things. First of all, it's easier to picture the giraffe and cow and what they're doing. Creating mental images is a very powerful way to remember almost anything. Second, because the words in our sentence bear some relationship to each other, they're much easier to remember. Go ahead, try it. See how long it takes you to memorize the sentence as opposed to all the signs. This method is especially easy when you remember some or all of the items but *don't* remember their *order*.

Remember: Make your sentence(s) memorable to *you*. *Any* sentence or series of words that helps you remember these letters will do. Here are just two more I created in a few seconds: **A** **T**all **G**irl **C**alled **L**ovely **V**era **L**oved to **S**ip **S**odas from **C**ans **A**nd **P**lates. **A**ny **T**iny **G**erbil **C**ould **L**ove **V**enus. **L**ong **S**illy **S**nakes **C**ould **A**ll **P**ray. (Isn't it easy to make up memorably silly pictures in your head for these?)

You will find that in business or the classroom, mnemonic devices like this allow you to readily recall specific information that you need to retain for longer periods of time. They are used to remember chemical classifications, lines of music and anatomical lists.

As effective as mnemonic devices are, don't try to create them for everything you have to remember. Why? To generate a device for everything you need to learn would demand more time than any one person has. And you just might have trouble *remembering* all the devices you created to help you remember in the first place! Too many mnemonics can make your retention more complicated and hinder effective recall.

Complex mnemonics are not very useful—they can be too difficult to memorize. When you choose to utilize a mnemonic, you should keep it simple so that it facilitates the quick recall you intended.

Many people complain that their mind is a sieve—everything they read slips through; they never remember anything. I hope you now are convinced that this is a *correctable* problem. You don't have to be a genius to have good retention—you simply must be willing to work at gaining the skills that lead to proficient recall. As you master these skills, you will improve your reading by increasing your rate of retention.

Chapter 10

Let's read up on ADD

We both fear and pity kids on illegal drugs. But we also must face and deal with what's happening to the three million-plus who are on a *legal* drug—Ritalin, the prescribed drug of choice for kids diagnosed with Attention Deficit Disorder (ADD), hyperactivity or the combination of the two (ADHD). I could write a book on ADD, which seems to be the "diagnosis of choice" for school kids these days.

Luckily, I don't have to. Thom Hartmann has already written an excellent one—*Attention Deficit Disorder: A Different Perception*—from which I have freely and liberally borrowed (with his permission) for this chapter.

Some definitions, please

What is ADD? It's probably easiest to describe as a person's difficulty in focusing on a single thing for any significant duration of time. People with ADD are described as easily distracted, impatient, impulsive and often seeking immediate gratification. They have poor listening skills and trouble doing "boring" jobs (like sitting quietly in class or, as adults, balancing a checkbook). "Disorganized" and "messy" are words that also come up often.

Hyperactivity, however, is more clearly defined as restlessness, resulting in excessive activity. Hyperactives are usually described as having "ants in their pants." ADHD, the first category recognized in medicine some 75 years ago, is a combination of hyperactivity and ADD.

According to the American Psychiatric Association, a person has ADHD if he or she meets eight or more of the following paraphrased criteria:

1. Can't remain seated if required to do so.
2. Easily distracted by extraneous stimuli.
3. Focusing on a single task is difficult.
4. Frequently begins another activity without completing the first.
5. Fidgets or squirms (or feels restless mentally).
6. Can't (or doesn't want to) wait for his turn during group activities.
7. Will often interrupt with an answer before a question is completed.
8. Has problems with chore or job follow-through.
9. Can't play quietly easily.
10. Impulsively jumps into physically dangerous activities without weighing the consequences.
11. Easily loses things (pencils, tools, papers) necessary to complete school or work projects.
12. Interrupts others inappropriately.
13. Talks impulsively or excessively.
14. Doesn't seem to listen when spoken to.

Three caveats to keep in mind: The behaviors must have started before age 7, not represent some other form of classifiable mental illness and occur more frequently than in the average person of the same age.

Characteristics of people with ADD

Let's look at the characteristics generally ascribed to people with ADD in more detail:

Easily distracted. Since ADD people are constantly "scoping out" everything around them, focusing on a single item is difficult. Just try having a conversation with an ADD person while a television is on.

Short, but very intense, attention span. Though it can't be defined in terms of minutes or hours, anything ADD people find boring immediately loses their attention. Other projects may hold their rapt and extraordinarily intense attention for hours or days.

Disorganization. ADD children are often chronically disorganized—their rooms are messy, their desks are a shambles, their files incoherent. While people without ADD can be equally messy and disorganized, they can usually find what they are looking for; ADDers *can't.*

Distortions of time-sense. ADDers have an exaggerated sense of urgency when they're working on something and an exaggerated sense of boredom when they have nothing interesting to do.

Difficulty following directions. A new theory on this aspect holds that ADDers have difficulty processing auditory or verbal information. A major aspect of this difficulty involves the very-common reports of parents of ADD kids who say their kids love to watch TV and hate to read.

Daydreaming, falling into depressions or having mood swings.

Take risks. ADDers seem to make faster decisions than non-ADDers. This is why Thom Hartmann and Wilson Harrell, former publisher of *Inc.* magazine and author of *For Entrepreneurs Only*, conclude that the vast majority of successful entrepreneurs probably have ADD! They call them "Hunters," as opposed to the more staid "Farmer" types.

Easily frustrated and impatient. ADDers do not beat around the bush or suffer fools gladly. They are direct and to-the-point. When things aren't working, "Do something!" is the ADD rallying cry, even if that something is a bad idea.

Why ADD kids have trouble in school

First and foremost, says Thom Hartmann, it's because schools are set up for "Farmers"—sit at a desk, do what you're told, watch and listen to the teacher. This is hell for "Hunters" with ADD. The bigger the class size, the worse it becomes. Kids with ADD, remember, are easily distracted, easily bored, easily turned off, always ready to move on.

What should you look for in a school setting to make it more palatable to an ADDer? What can you do at home to help your child (or yourself)? Hartmann has some solid answers.

- **Learning needs to be project- and experience-based**, providing more opportunities for creativity and shorter and smaller "bites" of information. Many "gifted" programs offer exactly such opportunities. The problem for many kids with ADD is that they've spent years in non-gifted, farmer-type classroom settings and may be labeled with underachieving behavior problems, effectively shut out of the programs virtually designed for them! Many parents report that children diagnosed as ADD, who failed miserably in public school, thrived in private school. Hartmann attributes this to the smaller classrooms, more individual attention with specific goal-setting, project-based learning and similar methods common in such schools. These factors are just what make ADD kids thrive!

- **Create a weekly performance template** on which *both* teacher and parent chart the child's performance, positive and negative. "Creating such a larger-than-the-child system," claims Hartmann, "will help keep ADD children on task and on time."

- **Encourage special projects for extra credit.** Projects give ADDers the chance to learn in the mode that's most appropriate to them. They will also give such kids the chance to make up for the "boring" homework they sometimes simply can't make themselves do.

- **Stop labeling them "disordered."** Kids react to labels, especially negative ones, even more than adults. Saying "you have a deficit and a disorder" may be more destructive than useful.

- **Think twice about medication**, but don't discard it as an option. Hartmann has a very real concern about the long-term side effects of the drugs normally prescribed for ADDers. He also notes that they may well be more at risk to be substance abusers as adults, so starting them on medication at a young age sends a very mixed message. On the other hand, if an ADD child cannot have his or her special needs met in a classroom, *not* medicating him or her may be a disaster. "The relatively unknown long-term risks of drug therapy," says Hartmann, "may be more than offset by the short-term benefits of improved classroom performance."

Specific suggestions about reading

- **Practice, practice, practice.** ADDers will tend to have trouble reading, preferring visual stimulation to the "boring" words. Turn off the TV. Minimize time spent with Sega or other such games. ADDers may well be extraordinarily focused on such visual input and stimulating games, but only to the detriment of their schoolwork. Where possible, though, utilize videos, computers, interactive multi-media and other forms of communication more attuned to ADDers to help them learn. There is a tremendous amount of educational software and CD-ROM material that may work better for ADDers than traditional printed books.

  However, ADDers must obviously learn to read and practice reading. I would suggest finding a professional or a program to deal with your or your child's probable reading problems. Anything you can do to make reading more fun and interesting should be explored.

- **Break everything into specific goal units.** ADDers are very goal-oriented; as soon as they reach one, it's on to the next. Reestablishing very short-term, "bite-size" goals is essential. Make goals specific, definable and measurable, and stick to only one priority at a time.

- **Create distraction-free zones.** Henry David Thoreau (who evidently suffered from ADD, by the way) was so desperate to escape distraction he moved to isolated Walden Pond. Organize your time and workspace to create your own "Walden Pond," especially when you have to read, write, take notes or study. ADDers need silence, so consider the library. Another tip: Clean your work area thoroughly at the end of each day. This will minimize distractions as you try to read.

- **Train your attention span.** ADDers will probably never be able to train themselves to ignore distractions totally, but a variety of meditation techniques might help them stay focused longer.

- **Utilize short-term rewards.** ADD salespeople don't do well when a sales contest lasts for six months, even if the reward is, say, a 10-day cruise. But stick a $100 bill on the wall and watch them focus! Those with ADD are not motivated by rewards that are too ephemeral or too far in the future. They live for the here and now and need to be rewarded immediately.

Chapter 11

Build your own library

"The reading of all good books is like conversation with the finest men of past centuries."

—Descartes

If you are ever to become an active, avid reader, access to books will do much to cultivate the habit. I suggest you "build" your own library. Your selections can and should reflect your own tastes and interests, but try to make them wide and varied. Include some of the classics, contemporary fiction, poetry and biography.

Save your high school and college texts—you'll be amazed at how some of the material retains its relevance. And try to read a good newspaper every day so as to keep current and informed.

Your local librarian can refer you to any number of lists of the "great books," most of which are available in inexpensive paperback editions. Here are four more lists—compiled by yours truly—of the "great" classical authors;

the "great" not-so-classical authors, poets and playwrights; some contemporary "pretty greats" and a selection of my own "great" books.

You may want to incorporate these on your buy list, especially if you're planning a summer reading program.

I'm sure that I have left off someone's favorite author or "important" title from these lists. So be it. They are not meant to be comprehensive, just relatively representative. I doubt anyone would disagree that a person familiar with the majority of authors and works listed would be considered well-read!

Who are Derek Walcott, Kenzaburo Oe, Nadine Gordimer, Octavio Paz and Camilo Jose Cela? All winners of the Nobel Prize for Literature (1989 to 1994, plus Toni Morrison in 1993). I'm willing to bet a year's royalties not one of you reading this has heard of more than one of them (with the exception of Ms. Morrison). So how do *you* define great if these award winners are so anonymous? I include this merely to dissuade another 200 or so letters castigating me for those authors or works I *did* include in these lists.

Some "great" classical authors

Aeschylus	Cicero	Homer	Plato
Aesop	Confucius	Horace	Plutarch
Aquinas	Dante	J. Caesar	Rousseau
Aristophanes	Descartes	Kant	S. Johnson
Aristotle	Dewey	Machiavelli	Santayana
Balzac	Emerson	Milton	Shakespeare
Boccaccio	Erasmus	Montaigne	Spinoza
Burke	Flaubert	Nietzsche	Swift
Cervantes	Goethe	Ovid	Vergil
Chaucer	Hegel	Pindar	Voltaire

Some other "great" authors

Sherwood Anderson	Maxim Gorki
W.H. Auden	Thomas Hardy
Samuel Beckett	Nathaniel Hawthorne
Brandan Behan	Ernest Hemingway
William Blake	Hermann Hesse
Bertolt Brecht	Victor Hugo
Charlotte Bronte	Aldous Huxley
Emily Bronte	Washington Irving
Pearl Buck	William James
Lord Byron	James Joyce
Albert Camus	Franz Kafka
Lewis Carroll	M.M. Kaye
Joseph Conrad	John Keats
E.E. Cummings	Rudyard Kipling
Daniel Defoe	D.H. Lawrence
Charles Dickens	H.W. Longfellow
Emily Dickinson	James Russell Lowell
Feodor Dostoevski	Thomas Mann
Arthur Conan Doyle	W. Somerset Maugham
Theodore Dreiser	Herman Melville
Alexandre Dumas	H.L. Mencken
George Eliot	Henry Miller
T.S. Eliot	H.H. Munro (Saki)
William Faulkner	Vladimir Nabokov
Edna Ferber	O. Henry
F. Scott Fitzgerald	Eugene O'Neill
E.M. Forster	George Orwell
Robert Frost	Dorothy Parker
John Galsworthy	Edgar Allan Poe
Jose Ortega y Gasset	Ezra Pound
Nikolai Gogol	Marcel Proust

Ellery Queen
Ayn Rand
Erich Maria Remarque
Bertrand Russell
J.D. Salinger
George Sand
Carl Sandburg
William Saroyan
Jean Paul Sartre
George Bernard Shaw
Percy Bysshe Shelley
Upton Sinclair
Aleksandr I. Solzhenitsyn
Gertrude Stein
Robert Louis Stevenson
Dylan Thomas
James Thurber

J.R.R. Tolkien
Leo Tolstoy
Ivan Turgenev
Mark Twain
Robert Penn Warren
Evelyn Waugh
H.G. Wells
Walt Whitman
Oscar Wilde
Thornton Wilder
Tennessee Williams
P.G. Wodehouse
Thomas Wolfe
William Wordworth
William Butler Yeats
Emile Zola

Some "pretty great" contemporary authors

Edward Albee
Isaac Asimov
John Barth
Saul Bellow
T. Coraghessan Boyle
Anthony Burgess
Truman Capote
John Cheever
Don DeLillo
Pete Dexter
E. L. Doctorow
William Gaddis
William Golding

Robert Heinlein
Joseph Heller
Lillian Hellman
John Hersey
Oscar Hijuelos
Jerzy Kozinski
Norman Mailer
Bernard Malamud
Gabriel Garcia Marquez
Cormac McCarthy
Toni Morrison
Joyce Carol Oates
Flannery O'Connor

Thomas Pynchon
Philip Roth
Isaac Bashevis Singer
Jane Smiley
Wallace Stegner
Rex Stout

William Styron
Anne Tyler
John Updike
Alice Walker
Eudora Welty

Some "great" works

*The Adventures of
  Huckleberry Finn*
*The Adventures of Tom
  Sawyer*
The Aeneid
Aesop's Fables
Alice In Wonderland
*All Quiet On the Western
  Front*
An American Tragedy
Animal Farm
Anna Karenina
Arrowsmith
Atlas Shrugged
As I Lay Dying
Babbitt
The Bell Jar
Beloved
The Bonfire of the Vanities
Brave New World
The Brothers Karamazov
The Canterbury Tales
Catch-22

The Catcher In the Rye
Chimera
*Confessions of an English
  Opium Eater*
*The Confessions of Nat
  Turner*
The Count of Monte Cristo
Crime and Punishment
David Copperfield
*Death Crimes for the
  Archbishop*
Death of a Salesman
The Deerslayer
Demian
Don Juan
Don Quixote
Ethan Fromme
*Far From the Maddening
  Crowd*
A Farewell to Arms
The Federalist Papers
The Fixer
For Whom the Bell Tolls

The Foundation

*A Good Scent From a
Strange Mountain*

The Good Earth

The Grapes of Wrath

Gravity's Rainbow

The Great Gatsby

Gulliver's Travels

Hamlet

Heart of Darkness

The Hound of Baskervilles

I, Claudius

The Idiot

The Iliad

The Immortalist

The Invisible Man

Jane Eyre

JR

Julius Caesar

Kim

King Lear

Lady Chatterley's Lover

"Leaves of Grass"

The Legend of Sleepy Hollow

Les Miserables

A Lesson Before Dying

*A Long Day's Journey Into
Night*

Look Homeward, Angel

Lord Jim

The Lord of the Rings

MacBeth

The Magic Mountain

Main Street

Man and Superman

The Merchant of Venice

The Metamorphosis

Moby Dick

Mother Courage

Native Son

1984

Of Human Bondage

Of Mice and Men

The Old Man and the Sea

Oliver Twist

*One Flew Over the Cuckoo's
Nest*

The Optimist's Daughter

Othello

Our Town

Paradise Lost

The Pickwick Papers

The Picture of Dorian Gray

*A Portrait of the Artist as a
Young Man*

Portrait of a Lady

Pride and Prejudice

The Prophet

Ragtime

"The Raven"

*The Red Badge of
Courage*

*The Remembrance of
   Things Past*
The Return of the Native
"The Road Not Taken"
Robinson Crusoe
Romeo and Juliet
The Scarlet Letter
The Shipping News
Siddhartha
Silas Marner.
Sister Carrie
Sophie's Choice
The Sound and the Fury
Steppenwolf
A Streetcar Named Desire
The Sun Also Rises

The Tale of Genji
A Tale of Two Cities
Tender Is the Night
The Thin Red Line
The Time Machine
A Thousand Acres
Tom Jones
The Trial
Ulysses
Vanity Fair
Walden
War and Peace
"The Wasteland"
Winesburg, Ohio
Wuthering Heights

Reading every one of these books will undoubtedly make you a better reader; it will certainly make you more well-read. The added bonus to establishing such a reading program is an appreciation of certain authors, books, cultural events and the like that separates the cultured from the merely educated and the undereducated.

Read on and enjoy!

Chapter 12

Reading: a lifelong activity

And further, by these, my son, be admonished:
of making many books there is no end...
                    —Solomon (*Ecclesiastes* 12:12)

Well, you made it through another book. I hope you found the motivation—whether intrinsic or extrinsic—to define your purpose, discern the important details, grasp the main idea and retain what you read. I promised not to preach about the joys of reading. And I haven't...too much.

Your need to read—and comprehend and retain what you read—will not end when you graduate from school.

Planning on working? From the very first week, when you're handed the company policy guide, you'll be expected to seek out the facts—like what happens if you're late more than twice.

You'll be required to read critically—and know what statements like, "Our dress code requires professional attire at all times," mean.

Business proposals, annual reports, patient charts, corporate profiles, product reports, sales reports, budget proposals, business plans, resumes, complaint letters, interoffice memos—no matter what type of work you do, you won't be able to avoid the avalanche of paper and required reading that accompanies it.

Not only will your job require the ability to read and comprehend, but so will other facets of your life. If you plan to own your home, wait until you see the pile of paperwork you'll have to wade through.

Credit card applications? Better read the fine print to make sure you know when your payment must be in...and how much interest you're paying on that brand-new TV.

Insurance policies, appliance warranties, local ordinances, newspapers, membership applications and tax forms—it seems like any goal you pursue in your life will require you to scale mountains of reading material.

For your own best interest, you must be prepared to read—and understand.

I wish you the greatest possible success in your future reading pursuits, of which there will be many...throughout your life.

Index

Improve Your Reading